6-11-10   gift

DEMCO

THE SIMPLE FAITH OF
MISTER ROGERS

THE SIMPLE FAITH OF
MISTER ROGERS

SPIRITUAL INSIGHTS
FROM THE WORLD'S MOST
BELOVED NEIGHBOR

AMY HOLLINGSWORTH

INTEGRITY®
PUBLISHERS
Nashville

Published by Integrity Publishers, a division of Integrity Media, Inc., 5250 Virginia Way, Suite 110, Brentwood, TN 37027.

HELPING PEOPLE WORLDWIDE EXPERIENCE *the* MANIFEST PRESENCE *of* GOD.

Grateful acknowledgment is made for permission to reproduce the lyrics to "Every Word You Said" by Mark Robertson and an excerpt from the poem "Custody" by Deborah Digges. Some quotations in the book are taken, with permission, from interviews the author conducted on behalf of the Christian Broadcasting Network.

Cover Design: The DesignWorks Group, Charles Brock; www.thedesignworksgroup.com
Cover Photo: Steve Gardner | pixelworksstudio.net
Interior Design: Susan Browne Design

Library of Congress Cataloging-in-Publication Data
Hollingsworth, Amy.
   The simple faith of Mister Rogers / by Amy Hollingsworth.
      p. cm.
   ISBN 1-59145-229-5 (hardcover)
      1. Rogers, Fred—Religion. I. Title.

PN1992.4.R56H66 2005
791.4502'8'092—dc22

2004022322

Printed in the United States of America
05 06 07 08 09 BVG 9 8 7 6 5 4 3 2 1

There are many ways to say, "I love you."
There are many ways to say, "I care about you."

FRED ROGERS, "MANY WAYS TO SAY I LOVE YOU"

To Mister Rogers and Joanne, his Queen Sara:
This book is my way.

And with special dedication to my father, Ed Christin,
whose bravery during the last months of his life
gave me the courage to pen these pages.

CONTENTS

ACKNOWLEDGMENTS

Thus I set pen to paper with delight.
And quickly had my thoughts in black and white.
For having now my method by the end,
Still as I pulled, it came; and so I penned.

John Bunyan, "The Author's Apology
for His Book," in *The Pilgrim's Progress*

If only that were all it took to write a book! The "penning" of it is only the beginning—or the ending—of a long process that involves many people, whom I eagerly take this opportunity to thank. My deepest gratitude to Joey Paul and Byron Williamson of Integrity Publishers for believing in this project, for inviting me into their family, and for being the careful custodians of what has become for me a sacred trust; and to Sue Ann Jones, a gentle lapidary, who skillfully refined my words and thoughts. To the Drs. Mintle, Norm (still the best boss I've ever had) and Linda, for their guidance and help; the Pastors Kniseley, Jim and Carol, for creating an environment that resulted in the idea for this book; dear friend Zan Tyler for her encouragement and prayer and very practical help;

adviser extraordinaire Steven Lentz for his wise counsel and unending patience; constant encourager and true neighbor Sandy Sullivan; insightful friend and faithful listener Renée Pleasant; gifted television producer Julie Blim for her inestimable contribution to our first visit to the Neighborhood; Brooke Boland and Sharon Sherrill for their generosity and friendship; Dotty Simpers, the David to my Jonathan; my parents, Ed and Carmela Christin, for life, for love, and for letting me unfold; my in-laws, James and Cenia Hollingsworth, for countless prayers and many practical helps; and finally, untold debt is owed to my three muses: Jeff, my muse of love; Jonathan, my muse of sacred song; and Emily, my muse of dancing.

A LEGACY OF SPIRITUAL TOAST STICKS

INTRODUCTION

THE REAL

MISTER ROGERS

As I was preparing to go to Pittsburgh to meet Fred Rogers for the first time, I had Uncle Al on my mind. Uncle Al wasn't my real uncle; along with his cape-donning wife, Captain Windy, he was an accordion-playing local legend in my hometown with his own children's show. I loved Uncle Al as a child and even appeared on his program with one of my five sisters. But then one day I heard from my friends in the circle (our unadorned term for *cul-de-sac*) that Uncle Al had chased from his porch some children who stopped by his home for treats on Halloween. Now, as an adult, I was getting ready to meet the uncle of all uncles, Mister Rogers himself. My childhood psyche quickened, dislodging the memory—and loss of innocence—that had occurred when I first discovered that people aren't always what they appear.

My childhood memories of Mister Rogers were less acute than those of my local icons. *Mister Rogers' Neighborhood* began to air nationally in 1968, and by then I was moving out of its two- to five-year-old demographic. More vivid than its public television début were the Mister Rogers parodies that emerged during my teenage years: spoofs by Johnny Carson, Harvey Korman, and, of course, Eddie Murphy with his now infamous "Mister Robinson's Neighborhood."

For many years I knew only the farcical Mister Rogers, the usually unflattering caricatures that made him famous for saying things like, "Can you say 'television set'? I knew you could." But when my two-year-old son discovered television, I was reintroduced to the real Mister Rogers, he of blue sneakers and cardigan-sweater fame. Making up for the mindless hours of *Barney* I had to endure were the thoughtful daily visits with Mister Rogers, the only person who could cause my whirlwind of a toddler to sit quietly for a half-hour. (My son affectionately referred to him only as "Rogers.") I've heard the same testimony from other parents who were amazed at the calming influence Mister Rogers had on their children. They said he was good for thirty minutes of babysitting so they could take a bath or enjoy a cup of coffee or talk on the phone.

For some reason it never occurred to me to leave my son alone in front of the television when Mister Rogers was on. As the mother of a toddler and a newborn, I needed a calming influence myself. Underlying the apparent simplicity of the program—the kind that was fodder for mockery—I suddenly saw a depth I had never noticed before. Mister Rogers was more philosopher than babysitter. And never once did I hear him utter the phrase, "Can you say [*insert inane word here*]? I knew you could."[1]

As a mother with a graduate degree in psychology, I also realized that Fred Rogers had a connection with children that went beyond his being kind and gentle. He had studied the cognitive and emotional development of children and

had blended his insights into an amalgam of wonder: what they could see with their eyes, what they could imagine with their mind's eyes, and what they could feel with their hearts. Philosopher, psychologist, and sometimes confessor—that was the real Mister Rogers.

My reintroduction to *Mister Rogers' Neighborhood* coincided with my eight-year tenure in Christian television. I had worked on a summer children's program for a Christian television network, and as a follow-up to that project some colleagues and I decided to do additional programming geared toward children. I suggested the idea of interviewing Fred Rogers, as did, coincidentally, another colleague. Our thought was, *Let's go to Mister Rogers' neighborhood and find out if he is the same person in real life as he is on television*. We also wanted to know how his faith undergirded his life's work with children. Boarding the plane to Pittsburgh, I was crossing my fingers that Mister Rogers wasn't an Uncle Al in disguise, chasing kids from a prefab porch in his Neighborhood of Make-Believe.

I soon learned that I wasn't the only one nervous about this meeting. Fred Rogers was nervous too.

LUNCH-HOUR SEMINARY

I'd like to be able to say it was my imposing stature or at least my journalistic prowess that caused him trepidation, but neither was the case. My five-foot frame isn't exactly intimidating, and my usual role at the network was as a writer behind the scenes, not as a journalist on the front lines.[2] It was the subject matter that mattered: Fred Rogers had never talked about his faith on television before. He had recently given his first interview to a Christian parenting magazine about his spiritual beliefs, but this was his medium—television.

Television was not the young Fred Rogers' first calling. His plan—and the expectation of his parents—was that he would attend seminary after he graduated with an undergraduate degree in music composition from Rollins College. But during spring break of his senior year, he received a sign from the heavens—or more specifically, the airwaves: Fred Rogers saw television for the first time. It wasn't the potential of the fledgling medium that struck him; it was its abuse. "I got into television," he told me during our first meeting, "because I saw people throwing pies at each other's faces, and that to me was such demeaning behavior. And if there's anything that bothers me, it's one person demeaning another. That really makes me mad!"

So mad that he opted out of seminary to start a career in television.

In 1951 he was hired as assistant producer, and later floor director, for NBC's network music programs in New York, including *The Kate Smith Hour*. Two years later, he was invited to Pittsburgh to coproduce *The Children's Corner*. On *The Children's Corner*, he stayed behind the scenes as a musician and puppeteer, reveling in unscripted banter with his coproducer and the show's host, Josie Carey.

Mindful of the need for an ever-deepening interior life—a contention that became a hallmark of his later shows—Fred hurried out of the studio each day to take up his seminary studies during his lunch break. As unorthodox as seminary-on-your-lunch-hour was, Fred also decided, when it came time to take a required advanced-counseling class, that he wanted to focus on children instead of adults. He wanted to "deepen" what he could bring to television.

He worked under the supervision of noted child psychologist Dr. Margaret McFarland at the Graduate School of Child Development at the University of Pittsburgh. (Dr. McFarland, who founded the Arsenal Family and Children's Center with Dr. Benjamin Spock and Erik Erikson, consulted with Fred for nearly twenty-five years on *Mister Rogers' Neighborhood* until her death in 1988. They were colleagues as well as revered friends.) Eight years' worth of lunch hours later, he was ordained by the United Presbyterian Church as an evangelist with a unique charge to serve children and families through the mass media.

Fulfilling a call to evangelism on a medium such as public television, which often steers clear of religious issues, may have caused some dissonance for both Fred and his ordaining body. At least one fellow student remembers the heated debate over Fred's ordination as a minister sans a church. Perhaps in an attempt to reconcile the schism, the ordaining body considered using Fred's talents to develop a children's program as an outreach for the denomination. Would Mister Rogers, yet to slip into sneakers and sweaters, be subsumed by Reverend Rogers?

The answer came, not through the airwaves this time, but through the telephone wires. First, he received a call from denominational officials to report the unhappy news that money was not available for the program they were discussing. The very next day he received a second call, from Fred Rainsberry, the head of children's programming for the Canadian Broadcasting Company. The closed-door-turned-open-window was Dr. Rainsberry's invitation to Fred to produce a children's program—fifteen minutes in length—to air daily throughout all of Canada.

Fred's assumption, upon accepting the propitious call to Canada, was that he would continue doing what he had been doing on *The Children's Corner*: producing, making music, and manipulating and speaking for the puppets. But Dr. Rainsberry had other plans. No longer would Fred be hidden behind the scenes, shadowed in a puppeteer's black shirt. No, Dr. Rainsberry had seen Fred interact with children, real children, and he knew Fred had a special gift. If Fred could somehow translate that into television—to talk to children as if they were there with him—the result would be more of a visit than a show.

By being called *MisteRogers*, the program would reflect the nature of that relationship, like the one a child might have with a trusted neighbor. And so Mister Rogers was born in that Canadian studio, and Fred Rogers had finally arrived—by a rather circuitous path—at his destined pulpit. He once told a fellow minister about his initial foray into commercial television, "I still wasn't sure I was being led."[3] But being able to use his gifts to nurture children through educational television was all the assurance he needed. There was no scarcity—even back then—of "demeaning" television, but Fred Rogers had refused to stoop to that level, and would, instead, rise to a child's.

PREACHING WITHOUT WORDS

During the report of Fred's death on the *Nightly News* program on NBC, the network where Fred got his start in television, reporter Bob Faw said, "The real Mister Rogers never preached, [never] even mentioned God [on his show]." And then Faw added, "He never had to."[4] Indeed, Fred Rogers and his gentle care of children seemed to embody the words credited to Saint Francis of Assisi: "Preach the gospel at all times; if necessary, use words." But when I contacted Fred in 1994 with the request for a faith-based interview, that's exactly what I was asking him to do: use words.

This may have caused concern for him on several levels; he was, after all, media-savvy enough to know reporters often come with agendas, and if he was going to "use words" about his faith for the first time on television, he didn't want them fractured into sound bites and wrapped in the neat little package that was more my view of Christianity than his. Nor did he want children who might watch the interview to feel excluded if he used words or terminology they might not have been exposed to because they weren't being raised in families of faith.

He didn't say yes right away; he mulled over the decision for weeks and consulted others—within his staff and outside of it—about what he should do. During the time he was thinking over my request, I opened my Virginia Beach newspaper one afternoon to find an op-ed piece by then-*Boston Herald* columnist Don Feder. It was titled, "It's a Psychobabble Day in the Neighborhood."[5]

In the column, Feder portrayed Mister Rogers as a man "with a Stepford Wives grin on his face, conversing with puppets." Of Fred Rogers' book, *You Are Special*, published in 1994 when Feder was writing the column, he said, "For over 25 years on his PBS series, Fred Rogers has been filling the innocent heads of children with this pap. Now he's instructing adults from the lofty heights of his tower of psychobabble."

The pith of his argument was that Fred Rogers advocated a philosophy of self-esteem that makes children feel good about themselves no matter how rotten their behavior or how dull their intellects. "If you want to be my neighbor, Fred," Feder concluded the piece, "you'll have to start teaching virtue and stop singing siren songs about 'good people who do naughty things.'" (The song he referred to is Fred's "Sometimes People Are Good," written to help children understand that they are capable of both good and bad behavior, as well as conflicting emotions and moods.)

That evening, while my children's eyes were heavy with sleep, having had their fill of pap for the day, I wrote a letter to Don Feder. "After reading your column," I began, "the conclusion I came to was this: right argument, wrong target. I agree that the cult of self-esteem has gone too far. What I disagree with is that Mister Rogers is a proponent."

I continued: "Mister Rogers, I would venture to guess, would disagree with the statement you attributed to him that 'judgmentalism will cripple a child's self-esteem.' Setting limits and exercising virtuous behavior are two mainstays of his philosophy. And with degrees in music, theology, and psychology, I doubt if he would agree that self-esteem should take the place of academics."

After offering proofs of Fred Rogers' position culled from things I had read about him, I concluded my letter: "Mister Rogers has stated that the guiding philosophy of his life is one he gleaned from a seminary professor: You can be an accuser or an advocate. . . . Unfortunately, Mr. Feder, your mean-spirited statements and fallacious conclusions have led you to be an accuser. Shame on you for attacking one of the few people who actually tries to do something positive for my kids."

Don Feder never responded to my letter; it's possible he never even read it. But Fred Rogers did. I sent a copy of both the column and my response to David Newell, Fred's public relations director, who happened to play Mr. McFeely on the program. I didn't find out until I arrived for the interview that this was the deciding factor, the thing that convinced Fred and the staff that I really cared about Mister Rogers. I was a mother defending those trying to help my two children to grow, not just a reporter seeking an interview. "How God uses things!" I scribbled in my journal that night as I was flying home from the interview.

A GRACE-FILLED VISIT

Once Fred Rogers realized there was no need to fear me, I was happily given the same assurance regarding him. I had the identical reaction to meeting him in real life as did author James Kaplan, who adroitly wrote for *TV Guide* that Fred Rogers is "more Mister Rogers than Mister Rogers."[6] There would be no chasing of children from porches on Halloween (although to be fair, Uncle Al's antics may have been the stuff of urban legend). I even found out later, thanks to his real-life neighbor, *Time* magazine reporter Jessica Reaves, that not only did Fred Rogers *not* chase children from his porch on All Hallows' Eve, but that his wife, Joanne, gave out much-coveted, full-sized candy bars.[7]

One of the first things Fred asked us (a fellow producer, the crew, and me) upon our arrival in his Neighborhood was what tie we wanted him to wear. He had three for us to choose from. One he called his "clergy tie," since it was a gift from a fellow minister. "I like to wear this on the program to give a subliminal message," he whispered to us and then smiled. He also showed us the reel of film that contained his first sermon. He said he had not seen the reel in years and had just found it that morning. "Isn't that funny?" he said. "I found it today, the day you're here."

I showed him a photo of my children and told him that my son, Jonathan, had expressed his first real sadness the week before, after watching the *Mister Rogers' Neighborhood* episode about expressing sad feelings. (Jonathan had said he was "very sad" because I had put him in a timeout, a detail I edited out of the story when repeating it to Fred.) Fred's eyes grew big at how quickly Jonathan had assimilated that information. "It will serve him well all his life," he said.

The interview went very well, with no cajoling on my part and no holding back on his. His faith, as I had expected, flowed naturally from our conversation. When we left, Hedda Sharapan, his faithful producer who at the time of our visit had already worked with Fred for more than twenty-five years, had commented that many requests are made for interviews, but only a few are granted. What made the difference with us, she said, is that we came in love.

Once settled back in Virginia, I wrote Fred a note of thanks, telling him about what had transpired when I came home: "I arrived home at 2 a.m. Thursday morning [due to a flight delay]," I wrote in my letter, "and tiptoed in to kiss Jonathan and Emily goodnight. A few hours later, Jonathan, my three-year-old, sneaked into our bedroom. He stood by my bed a few minutes until I woke up. I whispered, 'Mommy's home.' He was thoughtful for a moment and then said, 'Mommy, is Rogers coming to live with us?'

"'No, honey,' I said, 'but that would be nice, wouldn't it?'"

Fred loved the story; he quickly wrote back: *"Your story about Jonathan's asking if I was going to come and live with you all is so wonderfully childlike. How blessed he and Emily are to have you for their Mom! Thank you for your grace-filled visit to our 'neighborhood.' Thank you for your ministry in this life. Jeff must be very proud of his talented and sensitive wife."*

Fred Rogers was always saying things like that to the people around him: "How blessed your wife is to have you for a husband!" "How blessed your colleagues are to have you to work with!" "How blessed your children are!" (He once even told me that a magazine I was working for at the time was "blessed" *and* "lucky" to have me on staff.) But no matter how often you heard him say it to others, you never doubted his sincerity when he said it to you.

That was my first correspondence with Fred Rogers, after the big interview that almost wasn't. (Remarkably, when the interview aired, David Newell told me that it was the closest anyone had come to revealing the real Fred Rogers.) The letter marked the beginning of our personal relationship that continued until his untimely death from stomach cancer, a month before his seventy-fifth birthday, in 2003. (I received my last letter from him three weeks before he died.)

Dietrich Bonhoeffer, the German pastor and theologian imprisoned and executed for his opposition to Hitler, wrote in one of his letters from prison, "One writes some things more freely and more vividly in a letter . . . and often I have better thoughts in a conversation by correspondence than by myself."[8] That sums up my relationship with Fred Rogers, which flourished through the letters we wrote over the next eight years. We talked by phone as well, and I would visit the Neighborhood again, but the core of our relationship, our "better thoughts," developed through our correspondence.

SPIRITUAL TOAST STICKS

One of the things I enjoyed most about my friendship with Fred Rogers was the stories he told me from his childhood. It was Dr. McFarland, Fred's mentor in child development from his graduate studies, who noted that Fred was more connected to his childhood than anyone else she knew, that he hadn't "shed" the vestiges of childhood as most of us have. He was deeply in touch with the joys—and the pathos—of his younger years.

One of those stories, which he related to me the summer before he died, reflects his keen sense of both. For Fred, perhaps the earliest prototype of a true "neighbor" took the form of an elderly woman who lived in his hometown of Latrobe, Pennsylvania. She was his grandmother's age, and everyone called her Mama Bell. Many times five-year-old Freddy (as he was called) would amble up her back-porch steps looking for a snack. He would arrive strategically on her back doorstep because it led straight to her kitchen, where she often made him his favorite treat—toast sticks.

"Come for toast sticks, Freddy?" she would ask. One day Mama Bell asked Freddy if he would like to make the toast sticks on his own. Imagine his delight at being able to master what seemed like a grown-up task, as well as his pride at being entrusted with Mama Bell's specialty. He was prompted to put the bread in the toaster, allowed to slowly butter the toasted slice, and then top it off with a dollop of jam. Mama Bell even let him carefully cut the toast into four long sticks.

Very soon after that encounter, Mama Bell got sick and died. Many decades later, Fred wondered if somehow Mama Bell had known she was reaching toward heaven and wanted Freddy to have this experience as a comfort to him, as a reminder of their unique friendship. Even though she was gone, he could now make toast sticks on his own, and he would always think of Mama Bell as he made them. Toast sticks may seem like a simple legacy, but they had a profound effect upon a young boy.

This story was meaningful to me when I first heard it, but it took on special significance in the months following Fred's death. (I wasn't even aware that he had been sick; his cancer came on suddenly and took his life in a matter of weeks. But I had wondered if something was wrong. His last letter to me, the one that arrived three weeks before he died, was typed. He had never typed his letters to me before; they were always handwritten. I suspected that for some reason his staff had to be involved in completing that last letter. But at the close of it, in his own hand, he had written, *"Grace and Peace and Love to you all. Fred."*)

I thought about Fred and Mama Bell again when I returned home from his memorial service in Pittsburgh. Reflecting on our relationship, I realized that Fred had entrusted me with something very similar to the gift Mama Bell had entrusted to him; he had left me something while he was reaching toward heaven that I wasn't even aware of (although I had a sense that he was). For years—through our letters, our conversations, and our prayers for one another—Fred had left me with spiritual "toast sticks," a legacy that would comfort me long after he was gone, providing sustenance of a different kind. Now that I had them, I could enjoy them on my own, even when he was no longer here.

But Fred knew better than that. Sustenance is to be shared.

During my second visit to the Neighborhood, Fred was taping a program on sharing. He held a fig bar up to the camera and said, "I wish I could break this in two and share it with you." Later, during our interview, he said to me, "You know, we were just taping this afternoon about sharing. And as a matter of fact I was thinking of you, Amy, as I broke that fig bar in two. And as I said, 'I wish I could pass this through the television set,' it just dawned on me—that was very much like the Eucharist, how [food] could be broken and offered to nourish others. And yet there was no way I could put that food through the television set, so I said there are other ways of sharing."

Other ways of sharing. Other ways of nourishing. And so with that in mind, I began to gather up the spiritual toast sticks Fred Rogers had bequeathed to me.

My intention was not to write a spiritual biography or to take a comprehensive look at one man's theology. What follows is more akin to what is offered in another childhood story, not from Fred's childhood, but from one of his favorite books, *The Little Prince*. Written by Antoine de Saint-Exupéry, *The Little Prince* recounts the story of a young prince who has fallen from his star and his brief but profound encounter in the middle of a desert with a pilot who's been downed in his plane.[9] Even though both characters share the same plight—strangers in a strange land—the Little Prince is able to rouse what was dormant in the pilot, teaching him to appreciate life's mysteries through the eyes of a child. When it is time for the Little Prince to depart ("I'll look as if I'm dead," he warns the pilot, "and that won't be true"[10]), he gives these last words of comfort:

"And when you're consoled (everyone eventually is consoled), you'll be glad you've known me."[11]

Indeed, I am glad. Whether toast sticks from a grandmotherly neighbor or bits of wisdom from a wandering prince, everyone can pass on what he or she has been given by another. That's their legacy, and ours too.

I am slicing this book into several parts, much like a young Fred Rogers sliced his first set of toast sticks. There are toast sticks for the heart, for the eyes, and for the hands. Each theme builds upon the other to develop into a whole—a life of spiritual wholeness that's represented by looking inward with our hearts (inner disciplines affect how we see others), looking outward with our eyes (how we see others affects how we treat others), and using what we've learned practically, with our hands.

When I talked to Fred's widow, Joanne, about my desire to share Fred's spiritual themes, she recounted that he often made a distinction between religiosity and spirituality. What follows are examples of Fred's commitment to developing the latter, in his life and in the lives of others.

I.

TOAST STICKS FOR THE HEART

CHAPTER 1

THE IMPORTANCE OF TAKING TIME, THE IMPORTANCE OF SILENCE

And so, for me, being quiet and slow is being myself,
and that is my gift.

FRED ROGERS, DURING OUR FIRST MEETING

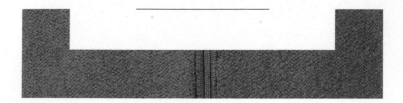

If you ever fall into quicksand, the most important thing to remember is this: take your time. Quicksand, unlike water, will not move out of the way to let you pass. Instead, it resists movement. Flailing about will only cause you to sink deeper. But slowly gets you safely to shore.

It's no accident that each episode of *Mister Rogers' Neighborhood* opens with a shot of a traffic light flashing in yellow caution mode. That message is the essence of every episode: it's time to slow down. The daily ritual of replacing his dress shoes with sneakers, his suit jacket with a cardigan, has, as *Life* magazine observed, "a way of lulling you."[1]

These days there are few proponents of slowing down, especially in television. Most children and adults are so accustomed to the fast pace and fast images that "taking time" seems like a waste of. The faster, the better. Even science bears out our obsession: you can break a thing's resistance the faster you push it.

But there are some things that resist hurriedness. Like quicksand. Quicksand, and other substances that react in the same way, are called non-Newtonian (because they behave differently than those substances Isaac Newton identified as having the properties of an ideal liquid). If you try to run your fingers quickly through a non-Newtonian fluid, the substance becomes hard, almost like a solid. But if you move your fingers slowly through it, the material yields effortlessly.

Mister Rogers knew that the same principle applies to a child's emotional development, to a child's soul. Hurriedness causes it to be hard and resistant. But taking time and going slow nurtures, or as he liked to say, "nourishes." (The adult soul needs this kind of nourishment as well.) I'm sure he wouldn't mind my saying so, but Mister Rogers was decidedly non-Newtonian in nature. His message was clear: Slow down. Take your time.

"I mean that when I want to do a thing, I like to take my time to do it right," he sang in his trademark song, "I Like to Take My Time."[2]

THE GIFT OF GOING SLOW

During my first visit to the Neighborhood, Fred was taping a series of episodes on *fast* and *slow*. While trying to show an appreciation for both modes, the balance definitely tilted in favor of slow: When Mayor Maggie sang "Peace and Quiet" too quickly, it seemed out of sync, ruining the natural rhythm of the song. Picture Picture showed that some workers, like crane operators, *have* to go slow to do their jobs. When the Trolley sped by at faster-than-usual speed, everyone in the Neighborhood of Make-Believe was alarmed. And Daniel Striped Tiger felt inadequate because he couldn't say his ABCs faster.

Mister Rogers knew how hurried children are in all areas of their lives. (School schedules may follow a fixed schedule, he once noted, but human development doesn't.) The episodes' themes were appropriate for my time there since the first question I had already decided to ask him was why he so often emphasized slowing the pace and taking time to reflect. Why was that so important for his audience? He paused, of course, before answering.

"I think, for me, I need to be myself."

Another pause.

"And I've never been a kind of a hyperactive, runaround kind of person. I think one of the greatest gifts that we can give anybody is the gift of one more honest adult in that person's life—whether [the recipient] be a child or an adult.

"And so, for me, being quiet and slow is being myself, and that is my gift."

(Sometimes that gift is lost on others. Prolific sci-fi writer Peter David wrote about seeing Fred Rogers on Johnny Carson's *The Tonight Show*, observing that even though Fred exchanged his cardigan for a suit jacket, he was Mister Rogers through and through. Johnny was so taken aback that Fred talked in the same slow, measured cadence that he used on his program that he could hardly hold back the laughter. "You want to laugh, don't you?" Fred asked Johnny. "It's okay." And Johnny did.)[3]

"It seems to me, though," Fred continued in response to my question, "that our world needs more time to wonder and to reflect about what is inside, and if we take time we can often go much deeper as far as our spiritual life is concerned than we can if there's constant distraction. And often television gives such constant distraction—noise and fast-paced things—which doesn't allow us to take time to explore the deeper levels of who we are—and who we can become."

It turns out that Mister Rogers' ideals are more than philosophical; his non-Newtonian bent can be quantified. Yale psychologists comparing *Mister Rogers' Neighborhood* to *Sesame Street* (which I also watched daily during my children's preschool years) discovered that children were better able to follow the stories on *Mister Rogers' Neighborhood* than the faster-paced, hip and hip-hopping world of *Sesame Street*. Another study concluded that *Mister Rogers' Neighborhood* led to an increase in "tolerance of delay," meaning that children in the study who watched the program were more likely to be patient in waiting for materials or for an adult's attention.[4]

Sometimes slow *is* better: in understanding, in learning to be patient, in "going deeper" spiritually.

I asked Fred if anyone else on television shared this distinction with Mister Rogers.

"Amy, this may sound like a cop-out, but I watch so little television," he apologized and then added firmly, "and I don't mean to be elitist about that. There are members of my family who watch a lot of television and get a lot from it. But I would much rather read. In fact, Joanne has been on a concert tour this past week, and I haven't even stepped into the room where the television set is."

Perhaps that was the essence of his success: He was a television icon who avoided the "constant distraction" of television. Instead, he opted to read.

STRUGGLING WITH THE TAKING-TIME TOAST STICK

I've struggled with this toast stick of taking time more than any other that Fred passed along. He admitted that he wasn't a "hyperactive, runaround kind of person," a term that more aptly describes . . . well, *me*. As a typical Type A who would rather eat standing up and who prefers to have all her plates spinning at once (like the guy who performed on the old Ed Sullivan shows), I excuse my behavior by saying I have what management expert and author Tom Peters calls a "bias toward action."[5] Fred was also a perfectionist (guests who appeared on the show were sometimes surprised to find that he wanted them to follow a script, not just ad lib. Children, he insisted, deserved something well planned and well thought out), and he was enormously productive in his life, filming more than nine hundred episodes of *Mister Rogers' Neighborhood* and writing more than two hundred songs. But he also fiercely guarded his time of quiet and reflection (as you will see in the following chapter), and he always, always took his time.

"Now [for] somebody who is naturally very effervescent," Fred added, while still answering my first question, "I would think that [being quiet and slow] wouldn't be a directive for that woman or man. That person would be best being herself or himself. Do you understand what I mean?"

And even though I did, I also realized that he had chosen the better way. But Fred was patient with me in the years that followed our first meeting. He taught me that taking one's time, especially in relationships, allows the other person to know he or she is *worth* the time.

A few years after this discussion, when I was in the midst of an exhausting move to a new community, he wrote to me in a letter, "*Just as it takes a tree a long time to begin to grow again once it's transplanted, so you can give your healthy roots time to find the nourishment of your new soil in your new community.*" Wise advice indeed, because, as a pastor's wife used to moving—and usually up for the adventure—this proved to be the most difficult move yet. It was taking longer than I expected to settle in, to find friends; I was frustrated and lonely. Fred always sensed when something was wrong. And he always knew what to offer.

SILENCE

Closely related to his encouragement to slow down and take one's time was Fred's emphasis on slowing down taken to its natural conclusion: an absence of all noise and distraction so that the only thing that remains is silence.

"We will make the whole universe a noise in the end," says the elder demon Screwtape to his nephew Wormwood in

C. S. Lewis's *The Screwtape Letters*.[6] While extolling the virtues of noise in destroying a believer's reverence for the things of God, Uncle Screwtape also tells his demon-in-training nephew that sometimes quiet can be used as well if it gives the person a sense of "devotional mood" while foregoing a real commitment to prayer. The reason this kind of quietness works, Screwtape explains, is because "it bears a superficial resemblance to the prayer of silence as practiced by those who are very far advanced in the Enemy's service."[7] The "Enemy" here is, of course, Christ Himself, since the conversation is between demons. But C. S. Lewis's point is clear: silence accomplishes more than noise, especially when it comes to prayer.

Fred Rogers was one of those who was very far advanced in the Lord's service and who often employed the prayer of silence. It wasn't just the absence of noise he advocated, but silence that reflects on the goodness of God, the goodness of what and whom He made. Silence to think about those who have helped us. He knew that silence leads to reflection, that reflection leads to appreciation, and that appreciation looks about for someone to thank: "I trust that they will thank God, for it is God who inspires and informs all that is nourishing and good," he once said.[8]

He used a noisy medium, television, to teach about silence. "I was halfway to silence . . . When I heard your voice," recited poet May Sarton on *Mister Rogers' Neighborhood* at Fred's request, since "Halfway to Silence" was his favorite poem of hers. Fred may have considered silence his most important legacy. When acclaimed musician Yo-Yo Ma visited the Neighborhood and played Fred's composition "Tree, Tree, Tree" on his cello, Fred took some time afterward to reflect. Let's take some quiet time to remember, he invited his television neighbor, to sit and think about what we've heard. And he did. It wasn't dead air to him; it was thanking the God who inspires and informs all that is nourishing and good.

Another time on his program he invited Sylvia Earle, noted marine biologist and explorer-in-residence at the National Geographic Society, to be a guest. The idea was to use an underwater microphone in an aquarium to demonstrate the noises that fish make as they're eating. The equipment was set up, the cameras began rolling, but the camera-shy fish refused to eat. "C'mon," Sylvia coaxed, "chowtime, dinner bell." The fish ignored her. Sylvia then told Fred that these particular fish are such noisy eaters that some people can hear them without a "fish phone." Still, there was only silence.

"Usually they have very good appetites," Sylvia said again, but the fish weren't listening.

What a disaster, most crew members on the shoot thought. *Surely Fred will retape the segment with a different aquarium and less media-shy fish.* But Fred didn't. Waiting on the fish was a lesson in patience, and he was instilling an appreciation for their quietness as well as their noises. If we can learn to wait through the "natural silences" of life, he liked to say, we will be surprised by what awaits us on the other side.

Fred always allowed time for silence (the older he got, the more he saw the need for it, he said): at the end of the myriad commencement speeches he delivered, while accepting an Emmy for Lifetime Achievement Award from the Academy of Television Arts and Sciences, in presentations at the White House, and even in Christmas cards (*"May you be blessed with moments of* silence *and* hope *at Christmas and always"* read his homemade Christmas card, with his own emphasis added). The thing Fred Rogers shouted the loudest was silence.

JUST BE QUIET AND THINK

During our second interview, when we were talking about the mail he received from viewers, he said: "There are so many caring people in the world. So many caring mothers and fathers. We hear about the other kind, you know, the ones who are always hurting people, but when we hear from people who will do whatever they can to give their children some nourishment, it warms your heart."

And then he abruptly turned away from me and toward the camera. He had the fervor of an evangelist, seeing and seizing an opportunity to reach a lost soul on the other side of the camera. "I wonder if *you* don't have somebody in your life that just the very thought of that person makes you feel better," he spoke passionately into the camera, to the person beyond the camera. "It would be wonderful if you could take a minute, at least a minute every day, to think of such a person.

"Just think. Just be quiet and think," he said softly. "It'd make all the difference in the world."

Then he turned back to me and said with quiet exasperation, "I just feel that there isn't enough silence, you know, and I'm always asking people if they can just give some silence. And we're in a medium that allows so little of that. The last time I was at the White House, I said, 'Would you please just have a half-minute of silence to think about somebody who has helped you become who you are?' and that whole fancy meeting, you know, that whole fancy East Room of the White House, sitting silently, thinking about people who they might not have thought of for a long time that had made a big difference in their lives. When that meeting was over, one of the guards came up to me all in white and with the gold braids and everything [he motioned with his hand, touching his shoulders], and he said, 'Mister Rogers, do you know who I thought about during that half-minute that you gave us?'

"And I said, 'No, who?'

"'I thought of my grandfather's brother.'

"And I said, 'How was he special to you?'

"'Just before he died he took me to his basement and gave me his fishing rod. . . . I hadn't thought of that for a long, long time.'"

The White House guard went on to explain that he was

very young at the time and that the bequeathal of the fishing rod before his great-uncle died had a profound effect upon him. In fact, he wondered if that was perhaps why he loved fishing so much and why he liked to teach the children in *his* neighborhood all about it. But it took those moments of silence—requested by Fred in the "fancy" East Room of the White House—to bring the legacy to mind. In fact, the guard had been just a year or so older than Fred was when Mama Bell taught him to make toast sticks, just before her death.

Looking back on that day in the White House, Fred saw the resurfacing of that memory for the guard as his (Fred's) main reason for going there. A great-uncle's fishing pole, a kindly neighbor's toast sticks, the gift of silence. Everyone leaves behind something.

PASSING ON A GIFT

Sometimes what Fred passed on to me had been passed on to him by others. Just before my second visit to the Neighborhood, Fred lost one of his dearest friends, and the world lost one of the foremost spiritual writers and thinkers of the twentieth century, Henri Nouwen.

I've often seen the awe that Fred inspired in people, but if anyone ever inspired that kind of awe in Fred Rogers, it had to be Henri Nouwen. Fred mentioned Henri to me often and was always encouraging me to read his work (a request I didn't honor until after Fred passed away). When

I visited the Neighborhood right after Henri's death, Fred was taping a public service announcement in his WQED studio. I was on the other side of the studio, trying to stay out of the way. "Do you ever read Henri Nouwen, Amy?" he shouted to me from across the studio. When I confessed I didn't, he said emphatically, "Oh, *you* would just love *him*."

Fred wrote about his relationship with Henri in an essay for Christopher de Vinck's *Nouwen Then* (in fact it was Christopher who introduced them). While discussing the importance of silence, Fred wrote, "Even though most of the world knows Henri best by his words, I've come to recognize his deepest respect for the still, small voice among the quiet of eternity. That's what continues to inspire me."[9] And then, at the end of the essay, he offered the reader silence: silence to reflect on someone who has helped or encouraged them, "perhaps a person who, like Henri and many of us, longs for deep friendships and reaches out to others in response to that longing—just as our God reached out through Jesus the Christ our Lord."[10]

And when Fred passed away, silence was offered at his memorial service for the very same reason.

June 29, 1997
Dear Amy,
Your beautiful note found me in Nantucket. Joanne and I have come for almost two weeks to get the Crooked House ready for the children (and grandchildren). We've been

blessed with the most beautiful days—clear skies, warm swimming water, and spectacular sunsets. In fact the sun is making its way to the sea as I write to you. Wish you, Jeff, Jonathan and Emily were right beside us this very instant. We'd probably all burst forth with the Doxology, either that or simply stand in silent wonder.

How good that you can show your children early in their lives the importance silence has for you. That will serve them all their days. May your heart and mind continue to be settled in God's tender care.

Love to all the Hollingsworths,
Fred

The importance silence has for me? I learned that from Fred.

CHAPTER 2

_____

A PRESENCE TRANSFORMED

BY PRAYER

_____

When I asked for your prayers,
I didn't mean to be vague about the need.

FRED ROGERS,
IN A LETTER SENT IN SPRING 1995

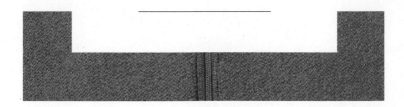

The ritualistic tenor of *Mister Rogers' Neighborhood*—the familiar wardrobe change in and out of comfortable clothes; the same opening and closing songs; the mixture of factory visits, make-believe, and perhaps a speedy delivery or two—was meant to make the children (and adults) who watched feel safe. When a young viewer expressed concern about whether he regularly fed the fish—she was blind and couldn't see him doing it—he quickly added a vocalization to his routine to assure her of each fish feeding.

You always knew what to expect from Mister Rogers ("I like to be told," he used to sing). The familiarity gave a sense of permanence, and permanent things could be depended on. Mister Rogers' graying hair and diminishing stature were the only things that changed over the years. Even the curtains stayed the same. Everyday ritual was important. When Mister Rogers left, you knew he was coming back.

Fred Rogers' real life included the same sense of ceremony. His daily routine was impeccably observed: he awoke at 5 a.m. for prayer, reflection, and Bible reading; took a 7:30 a.m. swim at the local pool (where he weighed in at exactly 143 pounds daily); followed his usual workday routine; and kept to a 9:30 p.m. bedtime. Even his diet had rite-like clarity: no alcohol and no meat.

It isn't difficult to see why a man with this level of discipline would be able to cultivate an interior life that would inspire awe in others. He once asked me, "You know how when you find somebody who you know is in touch with the truth, how you want to be in the presence of that person?"

People felt that way about him. I've seen cameramen on assignment in the Neighborhood moved to tears by his kindness. One woman even remarked to her husband upon meeting Fred for the first time, "I think I just had a religious experience." He had that unique, transforming presence: Mother Teresa in a cardigan.

Of all his daily disciplines, the one that contributed most to this transforming presence was the one that began at five o'clock in the morning. Slowing down, taking time, and appreciating silence are all foundational aspects of the next toast stick he passed on to me: the importance of prayer. Each morning he prayed for his family and friends by name, still offering his gratitude for those on his list who had passed away.

His prayers didn't end there but continued into his daily swim. Before diving into the pool, he would sing (out loud but not too loud) "Jubilate Deo," a song Henri Nouwen had taught him from the Taizé community in France. "*Jubilate Deo, jubilate Deo, alleluia* (Rejoice in the Lord, rejoice in the Lord, alleluia)," he would sing and dive in. He emerged from the pool ready to face a new day with a fresh slate, as if wet from baptism.

The prayers continued into his workday: "When I walk

in that studio door each day, I say, 'Dear God, let some word that is heard be Yours,'" he told me during our first meeting. Not only were his spoken words on television a focus of prayer but also the numerous decisions that had to be made daily. "*When I asked for your prayers,*" he wrote in an early letter, "*I didn't mean to be vague about the need. I always pray that through whatever we produce (whatever we say and do) some word that is heard might ultimately be God's word. That's my main concern. All the others are minor compared to that. As you know in this business there are countless decisions every day (every hour!) and I solicit your prayers for guidance from above in all the decisions which must be made all the time.*"

He continued his prayers when he ventured outside the studio. Sometimes he was invited to places in order *to* pray, as when he received an honorary doctorate (his twenty-fifth) from Boston University in 1992. The university had asked Fred to open the commencement ceremony with prayer. An older academic with a white beard rose to the podium to announce: "The invocation will now be delivered by Mister Fred Rogers." Before he could finish, the five thousand graduates went wild, whooping and hollering out the name of the man they had grown up with, the man whose daily visits convinced them they were "special." When Fred reached the podium, the tumult started again, cameras flashing throughout the crowd. How would he ever calm them down enough to pray? The answer seemed like the natural thing to do (to Fred at least). He leaned sheepishly into the mike and said, "You wanna sing with me?" And then chiding ever so slightly, "Why don't you just sit down, and we'll sing this song together." And so together he and his legion of television neighbors began to sing— in perfect unison, because they all remembered the words— "It's a Beautiful Day in the Neighborhood." Waves of red robes swayed side to side, arms intertwined, subdued by the sense of security and ritual that Mister Rogers had always given them. He was their robed curate, and their congregational response, uplifting and reminiscent, led right into prayer.

"Dear God, please inspire our hearts to come ever closer to You," Fred began, before praying for families, friends, and teachers. "We pray for . . . those people who know us and accept us as we are. Those people who encourage us to see what's really fine in life." Perhaps the graduates were thinking of Mister Rogers just then.

He moved from the particular to the general: "We pray for all the people of Your world, our sisters and brothers whose names we may not know but whose lives are ultimately precious in Your sight. With all our hearts, we pray for all Your children everywhere—yes, everywhere," he said, emphatically stressing the last word.

After praying for others, he turned the prayers to himself and to the graduates: "And finally we offer our strengths and our weaknesses, our joys and our sorrows to Your never-ending care. Help us to remember all through our lives that we never need to do difficult things alone, that Your presence is simply for the asking and our ultimate future is assured by Your unselfish love. In our deepest gratitude we offer this prayer. Amen."

RELATIONSHIP, THE ESSENCE OF PRAYER

Everything Fred Rogers did was a prelude to—or an outcome of—prayer.

Volumes of books have been written on prayer, perhaps because it's sometimes easier to read about it than to actually do it. But the essence of prayer is relationship, and Fred understood that. Even when he was explaining prayer to a young girl (I had asked him a question on her behalf about unanswered prayer), his seemingly simple explanation would enlighten even the most seasoned supplicant: "Now, you know prayer is asking for something, and sometimes you get a yes answer and sometimes you get a no answer," he carefully explained. "And just like anything else you might get angry when you get a no answer. But God respects your feelings, and God can take your anger as well as your happiness. So whatever you have to offer God through prayer—it seems to me—is a great gift. Because the thing God wants most of all is a relationship with you, yeah, even as a child—*especially* as a child. Look how Jesus loved the children who came around Him," he told her.

In another attempt to help children understand about prayer, Mister Rogers once took his television neighbors along for a visit to the Sturgis Pretzel House, founded by Julius Sturgis, in Pennsylvania's Lancaster County. The baker explained to Mister Rogers and the viewers (my then–three-year-old son and I were watching that day) how monks long ago gave pretzels as treats to children who had remembered their prayers. The dough was rolled into strips and crossed, to represent a child's arms folded in prayer (pretzel means "little arms"), and the three holes in the pretzel represented the Trinity.

Sometimes it's the simple things that remind us: dough molded into pretzels serves as a gentle reminder to pray; bread sliced into toast sticks brings back memories of the kindness of friends who are no longer here.

A COMMITMENT TO PRAY

By now I wonder if there has been a decision about your move. Please know that I've been thinking about you all. All that matters is your motives. God will lead the way. You know that.

Postcard from Fred, sent from Memphis on the eve of
another commencement, regarding our decision
to take a new pastorate

After our first meeting, Fred and I committed to pray for one another. The prayers may have started out as a sophisticated version of "God bless Fred" or "God bless Amy," like a child's litany at bedtime, but evolved into something more, due to the indispensable guidance of the Holy Spirit in our lives. These very special prayers, when each of us "sensed" the other was going through a difficult time, are outlined in the following chapter, which focuses on the Holy Spirit. But we didn't limit our prayers to one another; over time we began to trust each other with those in our lives who were also in need of prayer. Such a story follows.

In addition to those, like Fred, who know the value of prayer, there exists another group of people. This group—from noted philosophers (Nietzsche's "It's a shame!")[1] to politicians (Ventura's "It's a sham!")[2]—sees prayer as a sign of weakness, as a crutch for the feeble and weak-minded. To the statement "God will lead the way," they would respond that no, the strong walk freely, without support or leading. They would agree with eighteenth-century poet Alexander Pope, who observed that while rattles amuse the child, it is "beads and pray'r books" that are "the toys of age." He wrote, "Pleas'd with this bauble still as that before, 'Till tir'd he sleeps, and life's poor play is o'er."[3]

Crutches for the feeble, baubles to amuse in old age—prayer, they insist, has no place in the life of the strong.

Fred Rogers always wanted to be strong. As a teenager, he saved up his money and purchased a Charles Atlas exercise kit. Immortalized by ads depicting a skinny guy at the beach getting sand kicked in his face, Charles Atlas, the father of all bodybuilders, promised, "I turned myself from a 97-lb. weakling into the World's Most Perfectly Developed Man. And I can change your body too!"

Despite Fred's herculean efforts, he never came close to being the World's Most Perfectly Developed Man. The exercises did little for his frame, which he described as "weak and fat" at that age. (Perhaps it was this inherent sense of weakness that later helped him to identify so well with children.) And then in high school, Fred met another exemplar of strength in fellow student Jim Stumbaugh. Jim was the anti-Fred. Fred was shy; Jim was outgoing and popular. Fred hung from a doorjamb trying to become Charles Atlas; Jim handily lettered in three sports. It wasn't just a case of athletic versus bookish; Jim was also a scholar who made straight A's. In most worlds their paths would never cross, much less merge into one. But when Jim missed school because of a football injury, Fred took him his homework. That act of kindness, from an almost complete stranger, forged a lifelong friendship.

I first came to know of Jim in a letter from Fred in the fall of 1995. (I remember the letter clearly because he had written it on Friday the thirteenth and had scribbled "King Friday XIII's b-day!" in jest next to the date.) But he was very serious when he told me about Jim. "*I think about him all the time,*" he wrote as he told me of Jim's battle with liver cancer. "*If you are able, would you pray for him and his wife?*"

I heard about Jim often after that—his courage, how his illness had inspired his church to start regular healing services. Jim, who once looked like Charles Atlas, was now being wasted away by disease. His physical strength disappeared, but his spiritual prowess remained. *"He has used his long illness,"* Fred wrote, *"to help his church understand what real devotion means."*

No longer hero worship, this was one friend seeing the greatest spiritual strength emerge from another's greatest weakness.

Despite his strength, Jim lost his battle with cancer. Fred understood that sometimes God's answer to prayer is no. But he understood something else too: *"Jim gave us all an enormous gift by helping us understand the many forms of healing (not just physical) in this life."*

I learned about Jim's death through a message Fred left on my answering machine at home. "I wanted you to know that Jim Stumbaugh went to heaven on October 28"—his voice was slow and thoughtful. He rarely used the word *died* or the term *passed away* but preferred to say "went to heaven," underscoring the ultimate destination for God's children. "I had visited him [five days before his death], and we had such a wonderful visit together—he and his wife and I. And I just want to thank you for your prayers. He was an enormous influence in my life, as you well know. And I'm so grateful that you would have continued to pray for him. He helped so many people during those last years of his because he knew who was in ultimate charge. And the grace that flowed from his life into others' lives even at the times when he was the weakest was very, very powerful."

So perhaps the philosophers and politicians and poets

are wrong; perhaps prayer isn't a crutch or an old man's bauble. Maybe it's a necessity for both the strongest and the weakest among us.

WITHIN THE TOAST STICK OF PRAYER, A DOUBLE GIFT

In the postscript of the last letter Fred wrote to me before he was diagnosed with cancer himself (the last request he ever made of me) was a note about Jim's wife, Dianne. He wanted me to meet her, to contact her if I was ever in her hometown. He jotted down her phone number and ended with, "You all would just love each other!" (as he had been sure I would just love the works of his friend Henri Nouwen).

I reread the letter after he passed away, feeling a twinge of guilt for never contacting her. I was hoping to introduce myself to her just a few months later, at the family reception that would follow Fred's public memorial service at Heinz Hall in Pittsburgh (which would winnow down the twenty-six hundred who attended to a hundred or so). But when I was waiting in Heinz Hall for the doors to open, crammed in the lobby with the hundreds of others attending the memorial service, I heard a voice over my shoulder, a woman introducing herself to some people behind me. "I'm Dianne Stumbaugh," the voice said. I reeled around in disbelief. I approached Dianne without thinking and then told her about Fred's letter. I was finally able to do the last thing he had asked of me.

Dianne responded with the grace and sincerity I'm sure I also would have found in her husband, had I been fortunate enough to meet him. I was astounded. I had half-expected to be able to search her out in a reception of a hundred people but never thought she would be standing right next to me in a symphony hall that held more than twenty-six hundred. At the reception that followed (where I didn't see Dianne at all), I told one of Fred's longtime associates about what happened. She drew her breath in quickly and then declared, "God is among us!"

In the same letter where he first requested prayer for Jim, Fred had also photocopied a lengthy quote from Gerald May's *Will and Spirit*. This part he put a star and an arrow next to: "There are some things that are eternally reserved in privacy between the individual soul and the Creator. There is a dimension of delicate pain in this, but even in our aloneness we are together, for we each have it." And so with that Fred was handing down another toast stick: Prayer is not only a daily discipline that deepens our relationship with God; it also provides a way for us to be together in our aloneness.

Amen.

CHAPTER 3

THE WONDROUS WORK

OF THE HOLY SPIRIT

I've only heard Fred Rogers describe himself as judgmental once.

It wasn't a word typically associated with him; in fact, his character was more likely to be depicted by *judgmental's* antonyms: merciful, accepting, tolerant.

But at least one time he felt the word fit, and its sting changed his life.

He was in seminary at the time, during the eight years he juggled classes and his first program for kids, *The Children's Corner.* As part of his studies, and to encourage the development of his homiletic skills, he would visit different churches to see how the various ministers preached. While in New England one weekend, he and some friends decided to visit the church of a well-known and well-respected pulpiter. But after the service began, they discovered the presiding minister was away and a supply preacher—a rather aged one at that—would be speaking in his place.

That was, of course, a disappointment, but Fred had heard good supplies before, as well as meaningful messages from older preachers. Unfortunately, this man was neither good nor meaningful. Fred suffered through the sermon, mentally checking off every homiletic rule the man was bending, breaking, or completely disregarding. The sermon went against everything Fred was learning in seminary. When it ended ("mercifully," he later told me), he turned to the friend beside him to commiserate. But before he could say anything, his words were muted by the tears he saw streaming down her face.

"He said exactly what I needed to hear," she whispered.

That bungle of a sermon was exactly what she needed to hear? Fred didn't know what to say. But as he began to ponder the gulf between their reactions, he realized that the essential difference lay within: she had come in need and he had come in judgment. And because of her need, and the sincerity of the old preacher, the Holy Spirit was able to translate the words—poorly constructed as they were—into exactly what she needed to hear.

THE MESSAGE, TRANSLATED
AND TRANSCENDED

That experience shaped the rest of Fred Rogers' life. And it changed his Neighborhood as well. He not only committed to reserving judgment, but he also opened himself up to the mystery of holy ground.

"I'm so convinced that the space between the television set and the viewer is holy ground," he told me on the set of *Mister Rogers' Neighborhood* in 1994. "And what we put on the television can, by the Holy Spirit, be translated into what this person needs to hear and see, and without that translation it's all dross as far as I'm concerned."

An old supply pastor, many years before, had taught him that: What is offered in faith by one person can be translated by the Holy Spirit into what the other person needs to hear and see. The space between them is holy ground, and the Holy Spirit uses that space in ways that not only translate, but transcend.

"And [that translation], that's happened many, many times, hasn't it?" I asked.

"It surely has. Yes. In fact, there have been times when people have said, 'You know that program in which you did such and such and said such and such,' and I'll look back at the script, I hadn't said that at all—but that person would say to me, 'That meant so much to me.' And I thought, 'Well, happily, you got the words that you needed at that moment.'"

This adaptation by the Holy Spirit, as Fred describes it, has resulted in countless stories about viewers in need who have responded to the content of the *Neighborhood* episodes in miraculous ways. Thus a program not overtly religious, and for children no less, has resulted in a surprising number of "testimonies," typically a staple of overtly religious shows. What was not allowed, or perhaps not appropriate, to be communicated openly (because of the venue of public television) came through anyway and spilled over into these public responses to—and sometimes declarations of—the work of the Holy Spirit. When I asked Fred about these "testimonies," he said, "Oh, my, yes, some of the [stories] can make you cry. Some of the things that people have gone through, and yet they tell you what has been a help to them as they've been growing through those years. Some children, you know, are abused in all manner of ways, and here are people who have grown up and become adults even with all of those crosses in their backgrounds.

"And I just marvel at the strength of the human spirit to be able to come through real adversity, and many, many people will tell us that it was their faith that allowed them to watch us and know that there could be hope in growing up.

"I have a young friend who was terribly abused as a child. He's now nineteen years old. And his parents wouldn't even give him a winter blanket and wouldn't give him a bed to sleep in, and he found the *Neighborhood* and watched that program as he was growing up. His parents abused him so terribly that they were finally reported, and both of them were sent to jail. And this young man . . . finally called [an abuse] hotline and was adopted."

"How did the *Neighborhood* help him?" I asked.

"He said that it gave him hope. He never knew that there were such kind people until he tuned into the *Neighborhood*. And you know we do treat each other with respect, naturally. Everyone should be treated with respect, but somehow people [understand], *If it can happen here, maybe it can happen someplace else.*"

Children were not the only ones for whom this translation occurred. Some were Fred's own colleagues in television.

When Beth Sullivan was in her late twenties, she spent months in bed due to a protracted illness. She discovered

Mister Rogers' Neighborhood while flipping through the channels and began to watch it every day. The avuncular, almost paternal, nature of his television visits gave her a sense of assurance, and that half-hour became the highlight of her day. The Mister Rogers persona became like a father to her; Fred Rogers, the person, would eventually become her friend. Years later, as the creator and producer of *Dr. Quinn, Medicine Woman*, Beth invited Fred to appear on the program after she found out it was one of the only shows on television he watched. It was his only appearance on television as someone other than himself. He played a mentoring minister, a part that fit him like an old sweater and a pair of comfortable shoes.

For others the translation was more dramatic. Such was the case with Lauren Tewes, best known as Julie McCoy, the effervescent cruise director on the *Pacific Princess*, or as it was aptly called, *The Love Boat*. Lauren played the memorable role from 1977 to 1984, although *The Love Boat* aired for two more years after her departure. She left the show for personal reasons, one of which was her escalating addiction to cocaine.

I had heard from one of Fred's staff many years ago that Lauren had credited *Mister Rogers' Neighborhood* with giving her the strength to kick her cocaine habit, and I wanted to know for myself how a children's program rife with make-believe, factory visits, and music about childhood fears could somehow inspire an adult addict to find help. Lauren graciously shared her story.

"I was at one point in my life seriously involved with cocaine," she said. "I also made many, many bad choices facilitated by that attraction. I was [feeling], on one particular early morning at home, sad, frightened, and lonely. The television was on, and Fred Rogers' show was on the air. His signature opening touched me that morning, and I realized that in the world, there was someone who really would be my friend."

Lauren was a person in need, and it was for her that he prayed each day before entering the studio, "Dear God, let some word that is heard be Yours." While others may have judged Lauren—and she may have even judged herself—Fred refrained from judgment. He had left that behind in a New England church many years earlier.

"I didn't know at that time that that was God speaking to me through the instrument of Mister Rogers," Lauren continued, "but I had a glimpse of hope and moved closer from that day to a cocaine-free life which I have enjoyed for decades now."

Fred's intention was never to impose his beliefs on his viewers. Instead, he wanted to create an atmosphere, one that would allow viewers to feel safe and accepted. And that's what Lauren felt. Once the viewers experienced that unconditional acceptance, Fred reasoned, they could grow from there. And that's what Lauren did. Fred sometimes referred to his program as "tending soil." His role was to provide the soil, and he relied on the Holy Spirit to turn it into holy ground.

Fortunately, Lauren had an opportunity to express her gratitude to Fred in person: "While I was the guest host on the *John Davidson Show* for a week (many years ago), Fred Rogers was a guest on the show. . . . I took the chance to tell him of my gratitude to him for making hope a reality in my life. He was extremely gracious. I was born in Pennsylvania, and my older sister called me the day Fred Rogers died to tell me. She said we watched him when we were little girls and he was a local performer. She didn't know of my personal connection. Fred Rogers holds a warm spot in my heart, and I wish his family well."

Others for whom this translation occurred didn't have the opportunity to express their appreciation to Fred during his lifetime. In fact, Cathy Larson Sky, a musicologist and a musician from Chapel Hill, North Carolina, was so disheartened by her missed chance to thank Mister Rogers that she wrote him a letter—after his death. Her "Love Letter to My Neighbor" was published in her local newspaper.[1] Cathy's story began when she was in her late forties and finding it difficult to wrap up the work for her master's degree. She had completed the research for her thesis, but the prospect of committing it to paper—and exposing it to the scrutiny of advisers and colleagues—proved daunting. What she perceived at first to be laziness, she says, after applying for several extensions, grew to be "more akin to terror." Attached to the completion of her degree were some childhood fears about being the "smart girl" and some adult fears about the lovability of intelligent women:

"Achieving meant being disliked and sometimes being hurt."

Like Beth Sullivan, she turned on the television one morning looking for distractions. She found Mister Rogers.

"He was making a greeting card out of construction paper, carefully cutting pictures out of a magazine, planning how to paste them nicely and what message he would write.

"Then he looked directly into the camera and said, 'It's fun when you have a project. You have an idea for something you want to do, and then think about how you want to do it. It takes a lot of planning. I know it's hard work. And I'm so proud of you for trying.'

"Mister Rogers' gentle words sent a beam of light into the darkened room in my spirit where I'd been hiding in fear. I cried like a child that morning, snuggled in the La-Z-Boy by the TV, feeling old hurts melting away."

He had said exactly what she needed to hear, just as the old minister had done for Fred's friend in his sermon. Cathy began to watch every day.

"It was uncanny how the simple messages of acceptance and encouragement helped me to write and be productive. I would almost hold my breath while Fred sang his songs, for so often they soothed some tender place in my heart.

"When I finally graduated, I meant to send him a card thanking him for his help, but I never got the nerve to do it. In February, he died. This, then, is my love letter—a little late, but no less heartfelt. Thank you, Mister Rogers."

When I asked Cathy about her experience, she summed

it up this way: "I feel like he did such a wonderful job of aligning himself with love and compassion—[with] God, in a word."

Making a greeting card out of construction paper and a simple encouragement was somehow translated into the assurance of a loving, compassionate God.

If Cathy had had the opportunity to send Fred her "love letter" before his death, I wonder if he would have looked back over the script for that particular program (he wrote out each script in longhand on a yellow legal pad) and found that what Cathy heard was different from what he had said. It wouldn't matter to Fred; he would have just said again, "Happily, you got the words that you needed at that moment."

Fred knew that even more important than the words themselves was the Spirit behind them.

BETWEEN TWO WHO PRAY, HOLY GROUND

I just wanted you to know I was thinking about you, and you know our prayers and our love are with you all. Take good care, my dear.

Message from Fred left on my answering machine,
January 1997

Fred and I also had our own testimonies. We discovered that not only is the space between the television set and the viewer holy ground, but so is the ground between two people who pray for one another. The Holy Spirit can convert those prayers as well, even beyond words.

I mentioned in the last chapter that after our first meeting, Fred and I committed to pray for one another. It was another opportunity—as Saint Francis said—to "use words." A few months after my return from Pittsburgh, when my house had a rare moment of quiet (my toddler son and infant daughter were resting, and my husband was at church), I seized the opportunity to pray for Fred and his staff. (This wasn't the first time I had prayed for him, but it was perhaps the first time I had prayed for him free of distractions.) This doesn't happen to me often in prayer, but I was suddenly overcome by a rush of emotion and began to cry. I tried to "use words," but tears came out instead. I didn't know what to think. My husband walked in the front door at this point and was rightly alarmed. When he asked what was wrong, I hiccoughed like a weepy child out of breath: "I'm—praying—for—Mister —Rogers." I didn't say Fred Rogers; I said Mister Rogers. He tried his best not to laugh.

He comforted me at the time, despite his bemusement, but later joked that he would one day come home to find me travailing over the state of Barney's soul. I scribbled in my journal that night, "1/30/95—Wept and prayed for Mister Rogers; have no idea why."

I didn't want to alarm Fred about what had happened. This was very early in our relationship (and with my denominational background, I was more accustomed to these things than his Presbyterian background may have allowed), but I did mention it, downplaying the part about the sudden and inexplicable outburst of tears. He wrote back, as he always did, right away.

He wasn't alarmed. The day the Holy Spirit translated my tears into prayers had been a difficult day for him. He had undergone surgery for a recurrent and potentially life-threatening problem. "*Somehow you knew. Thank you over and over, Amy. I'm always grateful for your prayers. Obviously the Holy Spirit inspires your work and your life.*" When I read the letter, I cried again.

Another time I was praying for him, and the words from Psalm 92 sprang to my mind as an encouragement for him: "The righteous will flourish like a palm tree. . . . They will still bear fruit in old age, they will stay fresh and green" (vv. 12, 14). I sent along the verses with this note: "What you have done with your life has been such a witness to your relationship with the Lord, and I believe that witness will only grow stronger." But I worried about the "old age" reference; he was sixty-seven at the time, and I didn't want to offend him. Again, I shouldn't have worried.

"*Thank you so much for your timely note. . . . Yesterday the doctor removed a cast which had been on my leg for a month. Today I began physical therapy (a freak accident in Nantucket six weeks ago! I've used the pain and the time to deepen my respect for people with chronic disabilities) so I have felt really OLD."*

First surgery and then a broken leg—he might have considered my prayers a liability at this point. He didn't: *"Obviously you are very much in touch with the Eternal,"* he wrote, which is still the best compliment I've ever received.

But this wasn't a one-way prayer relationship. Fred sensed when things were wrong with me too. Like when I was struggling with the difficult move to a new home, a new church, and a new community, as I mentioned earlier. *"Give your healthy roots time to find the nourishment of your new soil in your new community,"* he had written, encouraging me to be patient with myself. Another time, when my husband was taking a sabbatical from ministry and working along with me for one of my freelance clients, the client suddenly laid off all his freelancers. The economy after 9/11 had caused his business to struggle, and everyone was laid off. Since the whole of our household income came from our work for this business, we were devastated. I hadn't told Fred about it (no one likes to announce bad news), but out of the blue came a letter from him, a letter of encouragement. *"Somehow I sensed that the Hollingsworths were going through some life changes,"* he later wrote.

During the fall a few years ago, I took a walk to clear my head and take in the autumn foliage. I was praying as I walked and also thinking of the concept of "true colors," as it relates to autumn. As winter draws near, the leaves no longer need to produce food, and the pigment chloro-phyll, responsible for the green color of the leaves, disap-pears, displaying the colors that were there all along: red, yellow, orange. I wasn't praying for Fred in particular as I was walking along, staring at leaves, but then a word of encouragement came to me for him. The encouragement was that even though he was at the age when most people are retiring from their life's work, a season of rest perhaps, what he had gleaned from his life thus far would allow him to choose something different.

"The fact that you are older now," I wrote, "instead of diminishing your impact upon this world, will allow you to break forth in a way you never have before. Perhaps the greenness of youth is gone, but in its place is a wisdom that allows your true colors to be displayed. I believe you are just now entering a season when some of your talents, those still hidden in your heart, will begin to emerge. It is a season of incomparable beauty."

At the time I thought that perhaps he would have an opportunity to share some of his spiritual themes, pass on the insights that had arisen from his lifelong commitment to taking time, appreciating silence, and making prayer a daily (and sometimes hourly) priority. I didn't know it at the time I sent the letter, but for three years he had already been considering retiring from the program to pursue other projects. Fred didn't get an opportunity in his life-time to share his spiritual toast sticks in writing, but it is my hope that perhaps in some small way, this book will reveal a glimpse of his true colors and the wisdom that was "still hidden in his heart."

TOAST STICKS FOR THE HEART

So far I have written about three of the spiritual toast sticks Fred left behind: the importance of taking time and appreciating silence, the indispensability of prayer, and the wondrous workings of the Holy Spirit in guiding our steps and translating the message. These toast sticks of the heart, as I have called them, all build upon one another: While taking time and appreciating silence are foundational to prayer, prayer is fruitless—indeed life is fruitless—without the direction of the Holy Spirit. These are toast sticks that deal with what's inside of us, our inner disciplines.

Cultivating these inner disciplines gives us the ability to see others differently—and how we see others affects how we treat them. To see others differently we need the insight of the next set of toast sticks, toast sticks for the eyes.

II.

TOAST STICKS FOR THE EYES

CHAPTER 4

THE BEST GIFT:

YOUR HONEST SELF

I don't think of myself as somebody who's famous.
I'm just a neighbor who comes and visits children;
[I] happen to be on television. But I've always been
myself. I never took a course in acting. I just figured
that the best gift you could offer anybody is your honest
self, and that's what I've done for lots of years. And
thanks for accepting me exactly as I am.

FRED ROGERS' RESPONSE WHEN I ASKED HIM,
ON BEHALF OF A CHILD, IF HE LIKED BEING FAMOUS

When *Life* magazine declared in its 1992 profile of Fred Rogers, "Nowadays, it's hip to love Mister Rogers,"[1] they were also pointing out that there was a time—maybe even a decade or two—when it wasn't.

It's difficult to unearth that sentiment now that Fred has passed away and his life work can be seen through retrospective eyes. The message boards dedicated to his memory are filled with heartwarming expressions of appreciation. But there are some message boards that reveal nuances of the other days, when it was "unhip" to love Mister Rogers. "Looking back," one reminiscent writes, "it is fair to say he was total cornball." But with the benefit of hindsight, the writer adds, "And growing up in a single-parent home, I'll tell you this: I needed the cornball. . . . I needed to know someone was there for me twice a day, for 30 minutes at a stretch, to devote himself just to me."[2]

Others who once derided him notice that over time their feelings have changed: "Sure, I made fun of the show when I was a snarky teenager, but when all is said and done, I would trust that man with my life."[3]

And still there are others who never "got" him but continue to try: "Since Fred died I've been watching the show before I go to work . . . [to] see if it's really as lame as I remember, and maybe try to tolerate my coworkers a little more."[4] Fred's influence is seen even in this person's reluctant "maybe try."

Of course in addition to the private opinions of "snarky teenagers" and those who thought the program was "lame," there were the very public parodies. While it has been widely reported that Fred came to view Eddie Murphy's "Mister Robinson's Neighborhood" with "affection," I know for certain that this was not his first reaction. To take the most essential elements of a person's character—his honest self, as Fred would say—which have been offered vulnerably, and to exaggerate and distort them in hyperbole is hurtful.

Given his nature, I'm sure that Fred eventually moved these farces to the imitation-as-flattery column. But what is more remarkable is that he never let the mockery or criticism change him, as those on television—and those of us in real life—are apt to do. (Who hasn't made an adjustment or two after an offhanded comment by a coworker or unsolicited parental advice from a neighbor?) But Fred stood fast. He wasn't tempted to change the pace of his program when MTV ushered in a generation of attention-deficient viewers. The set was perpetually shrouded in seventies décor, long after puke green went out of vogue.

Mister Rogers' constancy is what stayed with people. (This is a possible explanation for why studies have shown that children from lower-income homes, who often have to deal with inconsistency in their lives, showed a greater positive impact from *Mister Rogers' Neighborhood* episodes than their non-poor peers.) But for many people, that realization came only after they were able to look at *Neighborhood* through the lens of time; in the meantime, Fred had to resist the temptation to be something other than he was. And when he was asked to be something other— when he needed to wear contact lenses and heavier make-up during the last years of taping—he began to grow weary. It smacked of inauthenticity to him to exchange his glasses for contacts and cover his wrinkles with makeup. When he couldn't offer himself just as he was, he knew it was time to wave his final good-bye.

When I worked in television I had a colleague who produced children's videos. He said there were two elements integral to the making of successful children's programs: wit and heart. An example of a program with wit but without heart, he said, was *Sesame Street*. An example of heart without wit was *Mister Rogers' Neighborhood*. But to successfully capture your audience, he suggested, you needed both. Perhaps *Mister Rogers' Neighborhood* was devoid of wit and hopelessly unhip. But heart can go a long way, especially if the heart belongs to Fred Rogers.

THE MOUTHPIECES
OF FRED'S HONEST SELF

Many months ago I had a dream about Fred. We were riding in a van together; I was in the second row of seats, and he was in the third. I have no idea who was driving, but apparently someone was. Fred and I were in transit some-where, perhaps to an interview, and he seemed nervous. I reached back to give his hand a pat of reassurance when I noticed that to the right of him was a wooden arm, resting on the seat. It had a left hand, a wrist, and a forearm, with a metal rod at the end (for easy attachment, I guessed). Then I looked to the left of him and noticed that there was another wooden arm there, compatible to his right arm. I looked at him in bewilderment. "Sometimes I need these," he whispered.

Once on his program, Fred went to visit portrait painter Dianne Dengel, who had previously painted a portrait of Fred's father. Dianne had painted the portrait when she was a teenager, and because she was too poor to buy paint-brushes, she had used what she could: her fingers and lit-tle rolled-up pieces of paper. Now an accomplished artist, she continued to paint the same way. Fred was so delight-ed with the portrait Dianne had done of his father that he commissioned one of himself. When he went to pick it up at Dianne's cottage (this exchange was taped for the pro-gram), he found that the portrait was not of him alone; surrounding his carefully rendered face were all the pup-pets from the Neighborhood of Make-Believe for whom he spoke. Once back at his television house, he told the viewers that Dianne must have sensed that each puppet was an important part of what he thought and felt.

Fred Rogers' honest self was actually "selves."

The reason Fred "sometimes needed" the wooden arms

in my dream—or cloth puppets with plastic faces and immovable mouths—was because as a child, they had provided a safe way for him to communicate how he felt. As an only child until age eleven and often sickly, he played alone much of the time. And as a sensitive child, he tried to find safe outlets for his feelings, especially the negative ones. Later he would counsel parents to allow their children to act out their feelings through puppets, as a way to bring some distance between the children and their difficult emotions. As an adult, Fred continued to use puppets as extensions of himself; they became a way for him to take risks, to express subtler aspects of his personality at a careful distance.

Fred always said that the puppet most like him was Daniel Striped Tiger, the shy and very tame tiger who lived in a clock with no hands and liked to talk about "important things" with Lady Aberlin. Some of the important things they talked about were fear and sadness and what it means to love. Daniel often found courage to overcome his trepidation, and I wonder if Fred wrote his beautiful ballad, "Are You Brave (and Don't Know It)?" for Daniel. It's easy to see Fred Rogers in Daniel Striped Tiger.

Acclaimed writer and thinker Madeleine L'Engle once noted, in her treatise on the spiritual rhythms of life, *The Irrational Season*, "Righteousness begins to reveal itself as that strength which is so secure that it can show itself as gentleness, and the only people who have this kind of righteousness are those who are integrated and do not suppress the dark side of themselves."[5] Fred was certainly regarded as gentle, but did he have a "dark side"? He clearly understood the inherent nature of man. "There's the good guy and the bad guy in all of us," he once said.

And who were Fred's "shadow" puppets, the outlets for the subtler aspects of his personality? King Friday XIII was one, the heavily crowned and pompous king of the Neighborhood of Make-Believe whose idea of fun was "making pronouncements—long ones when short ones will do." I like to think that this affectionate bravado existed in Fred Rogers. He named King Friday's wife Queen Sara, after his wife Joanne, whose first name is Sara.

Both King Friday and Daniel Striped Tiger were puppets on his first program, *The Children's Corner*, where Fred wore his black puppet shirt and stayed behind the scenes. The show's host, Josie Carey, has said that Fred was so convincing in infusing the inanimate with his personality that she often found herself confiding in the puppets without a thought as to who was behind them.

And then of course there was Lady Elaine Fairchild, whose large ruddy nose, overly rouged cheeks, and suspect behavior frightened my son when he watched *Mister Rogers' Neighborhood* as a toddler (an admission he waited ten years to divulge). When I asked Fred if he named the puppet after his sister Elaine, he said, "Lady Elaine? Well, Lady Elaine is just about the antithesis of my sister. My sister is a real lady." He laughed genially and then added, "Lady Elaine is the chief of mischief in the neighborhood, you know."

I did know, and it's one of the reasons she's my favorite character. Her mischief—and her straight talk to the king, whom she called only "Friday"—made her the pluckiest resident of the Neighborhood. When she starred in a make-believe "soap" opera (complete with a bubble-making machine), she referred to herself, despite her warted nose and unseemly features, as a "froufrou heartthrob." I like to think Fred gave Lady Elaine her pluck.

Fred also animated other puppets with his many-sided personality: Queen Sara, the beloved wife of King Friday and the nurturing mother of Prince Tuesday; Henrietta Pussycat, who spoke mainly in "meows" (after Fred died, someone wrote in a guest book established in his memory, as if from Henrietta, "Meow, meow, sad day in the neighborhood, meow, meow"); X the Owl, who lived next door to Henrietta and sounded a little like Gomer Pyle; Cornflake S. Pecially, an inventor who lived in the factory where he made rocking chairs; and Edgar Cooke, the castle chef who always sang his responses.

Nurturing, soft-spoken, inventive, and musical: additional facets of Fred's honest self.

HIS MOST IMPORTANT QUALITY

But we wouldn't have known about Fred's complexity had it not been for perhaps his most important quality: vulnerability. Every day he opened himself up vulnerably to the viewer, not only through the puppets, but also through his other activities in the Neighborhood. I think he knew children opened up naturally and that adults who watched his program needed to recapture that ingenuousness. ("With children, you know, you don't have to talk about the weather," he once told me. "If the child trusts you, very often, what happens to be on his or her mind will just spill out. I remember a little boy in Chicago once saying to me, 'I don't wear diapers at night anymore.'" Mister Rogers engendered that kind of openness.)

There were times when his vulnerability on the program made me almost embarrassed for him, like when he tried break dancing or the Charleston or was so wobbly on rollerskates that he almost fell. Other times it was just amusing, like when he fumbled through a series of exercises, hopelessly mixing up the heads, shoulders, knees, and toes sequence and able to laugh at himself. But each example showed he was vulnerable; he was willing to try new things and keep trying new things even if he wasn't good at them. If Mister Rogers can be vulnerable, maybe even look foolish, well, then maybe it's okay for me too.

Even when he showed us something he *was* good at—his daily discipline of swimming—he demonstrated another side of his vulnerability. He wanted to show his television neighbor where he swam each day, so a camera followed him to the locker room and shot him as he took off his suit and bow tie (we saw him from the shoulders up, but we still knew he was disrobing). He donned a real swimming suit, not the long bathing trunks used for leisurely swims. He slid off the rim of the pool, and the underwater camera showed his pale body swimming to and fro, muscles lilting. He was all alone in the water: no cardigan, no blue sneakers—just Mister Rogers in a Speedo. The images were underlaid with dulcet music and were almost lyrical to watch, but equally difficult. You almost felt like you should look away, he was so vulnerably exposed; but that was Fred, laying bare his best gift, his honest self.

When Noel Tolentino, a twenty-three-year-old college grad and online magazine publisher, interviewed Fred, he mentioned that some of his peers were frightened of Mister Rogers.

"Did you say 'frightened'?" Fred asked.

Yes, the interviewer reiterated, one woman had told him that when she was younger, she was frightened of Mister Rogers.

"That is curious," Fred replied. "You wonder what she brought to that television set to be frightened by somebody who is honest. Well, maybe, honesty is frightening, I don't know."[6]

FRED'S LEGACY: RECOGNIZING THE LEGITIMACY OF FEELINGS

It's one of the important parts of the Neighborhood, knowing that feelings are all right. You know, that you don't have to hide them and that there are ways that you can say how you feel that aren't going to hurt you or anybody else. If there were a legacy that I would hope for the Neighborhood passing on, that's certainly one of them.

Fred Rogers in our 1994 interview

Many peripheral viewers of *Mister Rogers' Neighborhood* might come away with the idea that Mister Rogers was purposely one-dimensional and simplistic, for children's sake. I admit this was my first impression of the program. But the more I watched with my children the more I realized that simplicity and simplistic are two different things. In fact, if Mister Rogers was doing anything, he was underscoring the need for authenticity and acceptance of the complexity of human nature. For him, this self-knowledge was always the starting point. And one of the chief components of this self-knowledge was recognizing the legitimacy of feelings.

Shortly after I returned home from my second visit to the Neighborhood, my then–five-year-old son confessed to me that he had been afraid something terrible would happen to me while I was gone. I assumed he was thinking of a plane wreck or a traffic accident or some natural disaster. Finally, after much coaxing, he confessed, "I was afraid someone would think you were pretty and would want to marry you . . . and they'd never let you come home." I was dumbfounded; of all the things he had to be concerned with, he chose that—kidnapping and forced matrimony.

A few days later Fred called me, and I told him about Jonathan's comment. I thought it would amuse him, but instead he was very serious on the other end of the phone line. He reminded me that Jonathan's sentiment was very age-appropriate, that boys his age always think Mommy is the most beautiful woman in the world and want to marry her. (Fred felt the same way when he was a boy and even wrote a song about it: "Going to Marry Mom.") He also let me know that Jonathan's concern was less for my husband's loss and more for himself: *he* didn't want to lose Mommy to some other suitor. I had laughed off my son's concern, but Fred wanted me to legitimize it. My son's feelings were valid no matter how unfounded his fear was.

Fred was unrelenting in his desire to let children know it was all right to share their feelings—especially negative ones. Chief among the negative feelings he addressed was anger. Because of his serene nature, it's hard to believe that Fred Rogers ever got angry. When I asked David Newell, who plays Mr. McFeely on the program, what Fred did when he was angry, he told me that he played the piano, a coping mechanism he'd had since he was a child. I once asked Fred a series of questions from children, and one was if he ever got angry. He replied to the questioner, "Almost everybody gets angry once in a while, and certainly I do. There are times when maybe a light will go out, you know, or the microphone will go off, or something might happen at home. But do you know what I do when I'm angry? I like to swim, and so I swim extra hard when I'm angry.

"And also when I was a little boy, about five years old, I learned that I could go to the piano and play real hard on the piano, and that helped me; it really did. There are many things that you can do when you're angry that don't hurt you or anybody else."

THE GOOD FEELING OF CONTROL

Fred didn't advocate a freewheeling acceptance of any emotional outburst but believed that feelings should be expressed, and at the same time, controlled: "One of the paramount things I feel that the world needs to do is to be able to deal with the anger that so many people feel, and I like to think that the *Neighborhood* offers a smorgasbord of ways of saying who you are and how you feel. And we've heard from people . . . that say, 'I started to do something, and I realized that it wasn't right, and I was able to stop. And do you know, I thought of your song: "It's great to be able to stop, when you've planned a thing that's wrong, and be able to do something else instead, and think this song."'

"That good feeling of control. It's so scary for anybody and particularly for children to feel out of control. And I mean when Jonathan [referring to my son] is angry with you, there are things that he knows he can do like drawing pictures that won't hurt him or anybody else. What a gift you've given to that child! To let him know that he doesn't have to hit you; he can tell you in other ways." (I had brought with me to show Fred a series of notes my son had slid under my bedroom door one day to express his anger at me; one had a smiley face, X-ed out, next to his self-portrait with a pronounced frown. After I talked to my son about the notes and his anger, he slipped two more notes under the door: a smiley face, followed by a heart.)

"If the world could know that we don't have to put people in concentration camps and annihilate people just because we're angry with them. And the anger probably goes back for centuries. If we could just know that.

"Well, you know, I'm passionate about that. I just feel that we need to help children from the earliest time to realize that there are ways that they can express how they feel, ways that aren't hurtful."

Of course there are those who criticized Fred for his emphasis on expressing feelings, and for what the critics deemed was a wholesale approval of a child's every word or deed in order to ensure his or her self-esteem. (Recall columnist Don Feder deriding Fred for "filling the innocent heads of children with this pap.") But when I asked Fred directly about the oft-misunderstood concept of self-esteem, he said, "Now self-esteem is certainly not brought about by people saying that a child has done something wonderful when that person doesn't believe it. If a child just does a scribbling, for instance, or a painting with all kinds of mad colors, that child doesn't expect somebody to say, 'My, that's beautiful!'

"What that child is saying is, 'I'm feeling upset inside, and this is the way I'm expressing it. Would you please not tell me that it's beautiful?'

"Self-esteem doesn't come from a child hearing something that's not true about him or her. If an adult does not believe that the child has done a good job with something, well, it's not the least bit helpful to say so.

"Of course if we do believe that a child has done a wonderful thing, then the best thing we can do is to tell him or her, 'Hey, that was really special. You know you did that so much better than you did the last time, and I'm really proud of you.'

"I often sing, 'I'm proud of you! I'm proud of you!' Don't you with your children?"

I nod yes; I even use his version.

"But I would hope that you wouldn't say 'I'm proud of you' if your child has done something that might be hurtful to him or her or to somebody else, because that just doesn't help. I guess we're coming right back to the very first thing we talked about, and that's truthfulness—you know, being ourselves and allowing somebody to share in that."

THE STARTING POINT TO SOMETHING GREATER

If Fred's emphasis on taking time was the most difficult legacy for me to adopt, this is one that has provided the greatest practical and emotional help to my everyday life and family. Many of us grew up in families where negative feelings were discouraged or dismissed: "You shouldn't feel that way." When I was about ten years old, I heard my parents arguing (they assured me afterward that it was just a difference of opinion on "politics"). I was so upset that I wrote a poem called "When Love Is Gone" and slipped it under their bedroom door.

Perhaps embarrassed by my reaction, my mom encouraged me to write another poem called "When Love Is Here." This wasn't her intention, but the message I received was that there was no place in our home for my fears or concerns. Instead of dealing with my fear over my parents' argument, I was asked to write a sappy poem to cancel out my negative feelings.

This was a powerful lesson, one I carried over into my own family. Early in our marriage, I would dismiss my husband's concerns about problems. When our children were old enough to communicate, I would try to talk them out of their negative feelings—or convince them there was no foundation for them. But what I found out is that suppressing feelings has the same fate as trying to suppress a beachball in the ocean—they both come out sideways.

Feelings that come out "sideways"—in disguised forms that are sometimes more symptomatic than the original feelings—are much harder to deal with. It would have been much better to just allow my husband, my children, and myself to be honest the first time, to create an environment, as Fred said, that allows for expression of negative feelings. I still struggle with this one and probably always will, but I know Fred's influence has helped me to allow the members of my family to be "their honest selves." That's why when my son slipped his notes of negative feelings under *my* bedroom door, I knew not to ask him to cancel them out with new pictures of happy faces and hearts. He did that on his own, of course, but only after I let him talk about his anger.

Writer and apologist C. S. Lewis isn't known for his philosophy on self-esteem or his musings on the legitimacy of feelings, but he did make an observation about Christians and their relationship to Christ that I think Fred would agree with: "When they are wholly His they will be more themselves than ever."[7] Many people feel they must surrender their personalities in order to become more Christlike. But Lewis further pointed out that "the deepest likings and impulses of any man are the raw material, the starting-point, with which [Christ] has furnished him."[8] Surrendering our lives is not the same as relinquishing our God-given personalities. When we are in Christ, we will be more ourselves than ever. Encouraging others to be themselves, their honest selves, was the hallmark of Fred's ministry here on earth. It was *the best gift* he could offer.

That doesn't mean he advocated a false sense of self-worth or that he refrained from challenging others to grow. (His attempts to stretch me spiritually once prompted me to write him a letter I'm now embarrassed by. That confession is in the following chapter.) Fred rightly reasoned that if we accept ourselves we are better equipped to accept our neighbor. So accepting ourselves is always the starting point to something greater—a deeper maturity, a deeper walk with the Lord, and ultimately, a greater acceptance and understanding of our neighbor. This is the first of the toast sticks for the eyes: How we see ourselves affects how we see others.

CHAPTER 5

WHO IS MY NEIGHBOR?

Know this: You should judge every person by his merits. Even someone who seems completely wicked, you must search and find that little speck of good, for in that place, he is not wicked. By this you will raise him up, and help him return to G-d. And you must also do this for yourself, finding your own good points, one after the other, and raising yourself up. This is how melodies are made, note after note.

REBBE NACHMAN OF BRESLOV

When you live in a town of one hundred people, it's usually not necessary to look out the window to check who's there before opening the front door (especially when, for most people in a small town, the front door is rarely used. Everyone knows to come in the back door, and knocking first is an optional courtesy). So when I heard the loud rap on the front door that morning, I didn't bother to look. Instead I swung open the door and caught sight of a tall, thin man I didn't recognize. He was dressed in mud-splattered coveralls with hair that looked like he had just awoken from a weeklong nap. His gaze was slightly vacuous. There was a splattering noise at his feet. If Jesus had asked me at that moment who my neighbor was, I would have pleaded, "Anyone but this man."

I stood frozen for a few seconds as I looked from the red-black puddle at his feet to the large cut of raw meat dripping blood through his fingers. He reached out his hands, and now the blood was dripping on the welcome mat that greeted visitors to the parsonage. "This is for you," he said, looking down and avoiding my widening eyes.

That was the first time I met Junior. My husband was pastoring a small rural church at the time, and we were enjoying the slow pace of the country in contrast to the bustle of the city we had just left. Usually when there was a knock at the door, it was someone with fresh vegetables from their garden, their "firstfruits" offering to the pastor. But this time it was Junior.

Junior was a bona fide hermit. Except for when he sold the vegetables from his garden to townsfolk or did piecemeal work for local farmers, he rarely had contact with people. A fiftyish bachelor who looked older than he was, Junior lived alone in a dilapidated house that slanted sideways and rested upon dirt floors. It was rumored that electricity and indoor plumbing were modern concoctions he could do without. Junior had worked as a farmhand for one of our deacons and had recently suffered a stroke. At the request of the deacon, my husband had gone to visit and pray with Junior in the hospital, and to show his appreciation, Junior had brought us a gift, venison in its most rudimentary state.

BE THE GOOD NEIGHBOR

When an expert in the law tested Jesus by asking Him what he had to do to inherit eternal life, Jesus answered him—as He often did—with a question: "What is written in the Law?"

The man replied, "'Love the Lord your God with all your heart and with all your soul and with all your strength and with all your mind'; and, 'Love your neighbor as yourself'" (Luke 10:27).

When Jesus confirmed his answer, the man probed further: "And who is my neighbor?"

This time Jesus answered with a parable: A man traveling from Jerusalem to Jericho is waylaid by robbers, stripped, beaten, and left for dead. A priest traveling along the same road sees the man but passes on the other side. A Levite, later traveling on the road, does the same. But a Samaritan (an unexpected plot twist given the bitter hostility between the Jews and the Samaritans, who were a mixed-blood race) "took pity on him." The Samaritan tended to the man's wounds, took him to an inn, and cared for him. He paid the innkeeper enough money to keep the man for two months and promised to reimburse the innkeeper for any extra expenses when he returned.

After telling the story, Jesus asked, "Which of these three do you think was a neighbor to the man who fell into the hands of robbers?"

The expert of the law replied, "The one who had mercy on him."

"Go and do likewise," Jesus said. He made it clear that it's less about determining who your neighbor is (i.e., who it is you're supposed to love, according to the biblical command) and more about establishing yourself as a neighbor by your show of mercy to others. Jesus transformed the question "Who is my neighbor?" into the directive "Be the good neighbor."

If there is a central biblical theme to *Mister Rogers' Neighborhood*, this is it. The program wasn't named after Mister Rogers alone but after his community of neighbors. "I'd like for you to know my television neighbor,"

Fred said to frequent guests as he looked into the camera at his audience. His definition of *neighbor* was simple: the person you happen to be with at the moment—whether that person is a Samaritan, a hermit bearing gifts, or a television viewer. This is even more the case if the person you happen to be with is in need, as was the waylaid traveler in Jesus' parable.

At the center of Fred's theology of loving your neighbor was this: Every person is made in the image of God, and for that reason alone, he or she is to be valued—"appreciated," he liked to say. He believed there is sacredness in all creation—including fallen man—because of one Man, "the true light, which enlightens everyone" (John 1:9, NRSV).

"It is God who inspires and informs all that is nourishing and good" in this world, Fred once said. He was less a proponent of hymn writer Isaac Watts's view of man— "such a worm as I"—and more a proponent of hymn writer Maltbie D. Babcock's view of God: "[My Father] shines in all that's fair." Fred believed there are those in our world, people his mother called "helpers," who allow us to remember what is good about being human. Even God chose to identify with being human, he once noted, and He continues to work through those created in His image.

I suspect that some of Fred's understanding of what it means to be a neighbor grew out of the work of Benedictine monks who planted their first American monastery right in Fred's backyard, his hometown of Latrobe, Pennsylvania. Monks from Saint Vincent Archabbey (which now operates Saint Vincent College and Saint Vincent Seminary) used to visit his grandparents and parents, and the arch-abbey's pride in its native son is evident in a center at Saint Vincent College recently named after Fred and dedicated to continuing his advocacy in early childhood learning and children's media.

It was through the monks and *their* work in his community of neighbors that a young Fred Rogers learned to heed Saint Benedict's call to respect and revere the whole of God's creation because "the divine presence is everywhere." And because the divine presence is everywhere, the Benedictine rule reads, "and the eyes of the Lord behold the good and bad in every place [adapted from Proverbs 15:3], let us firmly believe this, especially when we take part in the Work of God."[1] For Fred, and for Mister Rogers, this was the work of God: seeing the eternal in your neighbor, that divine presence that allows us to show mercy to our neighbor—and to receive it.

SEEING WHAT'S WONDERFUL ABOUT OUR NEIGHBOR

The foundation for Fred's understanding of *neighbor* as an adult came from his beloved professor Dr. William Orr. Dr. Orr taught at the seminary Fred attended during his early years in television. "I signed up for every course he ever gave," Fred told me. "I didn't care what it was; it could have been canoeing, and I would have signed up for it." It was of Dr. Orr that he had said, "You know how when you find somebody who you know is in touch with the truth, how you want to be in the presence of that person?" Fred felt that way about Dr. Orr, just as others would come to feel about Fred.

Dr. Orr taught him that on one side of the spectrum stood the evil one, the accuser. In explaining what he had learned from his mentor, Fred told me, "Evil would like nothing better than to have us feel awful about who we are. And that would be back in here [in our minds], and we'd look through those eyes at our neighbor, and see only what's awful—in fact, *look* for what's awful in our neighbor."

On the other side of the accuser stood Jesus, our advocate. "But Jesus would want us to feel as good as possible about God's creation within us," Fred said, "and in here [in our minds], we would look through those eyes, and see what's wonderful about our neighbor. I often think about that."

No matter how ill conceived Junior's show of appreciation was, he became my neighbor that day. He came to visit a second time, thankfully without a recently departed gift, and was standing in the living room, looking at an old painting I had just bought. I hadn't bothered to replace the cracked glass or refurbish the frame in any way; I liked it worn, still bearing the nicks and scuffs of time. My daughter, Emily, who was four at the time, watched Junior as he looked at the painting. Emily has always had an ethereal quality about her, as if she has a spiritual awareness of things most others aren't privy to and a deep compassion for anyone who is hurting. "My Mommy likes broken things," she said, her eyes moving from the painting to Junior, and then she added, "like you."

Junior *had* been broken by life, and like my distressed frame, no one had bothered to try to repair him. From what we could gather, his parents had either died or left him when he was a boy, and he had been raised by an uncle who had since died, leaving him completely alone. I wonder if my husband was the only visitor who came to see him in the hospital when he suffered a stroke. My husband had found him paging through a Gideon's Bible left in the hospital nightstand. Junior's sudden interest in his own mortality led to further conversation, and together my husband and Junior prayed for new life, eternal life.

A few months after our first meeting, we asked Junior to spend Christmas with us. When I greeted him at the door, the coveralls had been replaced by an old suit jacket, a few sizes too small, his long arms stretching beyond the jacket sleeves, which were ripped in the elbows. He had carefully smoothed down his hair. His wanting to dress up for our celebration deeply touched me; he was the most resplendent Christmas guest we'd ever had. He didn't eat much and left early after complaining of not feeling well, but his presence was the best part of the day for me. "Last night when I lay in bed," I wrote in my journal the next day, "I sensed the Lord giving us a gentle thank you for ministering and feeding Him on Christmas day. That was Jesus Himself in Junior's chair."

I wrote Fred about our yuletide blessing, and he quickly wrote back, *"How wonderful to hear of your and Jeff's relationship with Junior. Isn't it just like God to surprise you all by giving you such an unexpected gift? The fact that you felt honored by Junior's being with you for Christmas is the greatest gift you could have given to him."*

Our experience with Junior had been timely for Fred, who had just ordered a copy of a lecture for me, one that offered a spiritual explanation for our unlikely kinship with Junior. *"When I heard this recording I thought of you,"* he wrote, *"so I sent for a copy for you. I hope that you and Jeff might be able to find an uninterrupted hour some time to listen to it. You may be thinking of Junior [while you listen to it]."*

It's difficult to explain the impact the lecture, delivered by a scholarly author and sponsored by the Chautauqua Institution, had on me, but it's fair to say it wasn't the impact Fred had intended. As I look back on the incident with the clarity of hindsight, I realize what he was trying to do. There was some rigidity in my spiritual thought he was trying to unloose, but he nudged before I was ready. Determined to set him straight, I shut off the cassette player and started to write my response to him: "I think you may be surprised to discover that I found much of her lecture unsettling," I began. I continued to tear away at the speaker's theology, completely missing the point of the lecture.

Even though I have only heard Fred describe himself as judgmental once, my track record isn't quite as good. My reaction to the lecture Fred had taken the time to purchase and send to me added one more tick to that column. (One of Fred's favorite writers, Frederick Buechner, once asked, "Would I have cringed [at my earlier writings] the way you can cringe at letters you wrote long ago, wondering how on earth you could ever have been so callow and wrongheaded, so alternately glib and pontifical?"[2] That's how I feel about this letter.) After mercilessly berating the speaker, I concluded with an unconvincing, "Thank you for giving me the opportunity to exercise my mind."

Fred's response was immediate: "*You're such a gracious person,*" he wrote. (The words still sting my captious heart, even today.) "*Allowing [the speaker's] lecture . . . to 'exercise your mind' is exactly what it's meant to do, I feel. Her relationship with the living God probably brings her to the conclusion she comes to about the essence of all religion. That's what impressed me. And that's what's of prime importance about your work and Jeff's work, i.e., finding 'the divine sacredness and otherness and holiness that we find in God in our neighbor.' That's what you've done with Junior and that's what he was able to come to do with you. Jubilate Deo!*"

Time has helped me to see that Fred was only saying, and the lecturer was only saying, the very thing I had written in my journal: Junior had represented Christ to us, and by caring for him, "the least of these" (Matthew 25:40), we were caring for Christ. But I was too offended by the speaker's theological leanings, so different from my own, to see that clearly. Toward the end of the lecture, she referred to the estrangement between biblical twins Jacob and Esau, concluding with their reconciliation on the plains of ancient Israel. Esau's favorable reception of his brother (he ran to meet Jacob, threw his arms around his neck, and kissed him) led Jacob to exclaim, "For to see your face is like seeing the face of God." (Genesis 33:10).

Her main point, the pearl I wasn't able to scrape from the muck of the oyster at the time, was that we should all see the face of God in each other. And this recognition manifests itself in acts of loving and practical compassion—like the gifts Jacob offered Esau—toward not only our brother but our neighbor. Fred, in his gentle response, was only asking me to dig a little deeper for the pearl.

"NAMING" YOUR NEIGHBOR

[I]f your name isn't known, then it's a very lonely feeling.

Madeleine L'Engle, *A Wind in the Door*

Esteemed author Madeleine L'Engle, in the second of her Time Quartet books, *A Wind in the Door*, issues a challenge to the young heroine, Meg Murry—first introduced in the staple of required reading lists, *A Wrinkle in Time*. The challenge comes through cherubim, represented in the single character Proginoskes (Progo for short), sent to enlist Meg's help in the cosmic battle between good and evil. Meg's task—her challenge—Progo tells her, is to be a "Namer." When Meg asks the angel what that means, he fumes, "I've *told* you. A Namer has to know who people are, and who they are meant to be."[3]

As in any war, the enemy has the opposite goal. In this case, the enemies are Echthroi, evil forces and fallen angels, whose chief weapon is un-Naming, "making people not know who they are."

"When people don't know who they are," Progo explains, "they are open to being Xed [annihilated by hate], or Named."[4] Or, as Fred Rogers' beloved Dr. Orr would say, they become either accusers or advocates.

"If someone knows who he is, really knows," the cherubim explains, "then he doesn't need to hate."[5] Fred would agree: feeling as good as possible about God's creation within us, he believed, causes us to look upon our neighbor with the same sense of wonder and worth.

Then, once we are able to see the image of God in our neighbors, once we recognize their inherent value, we strive to help them become who they are meant to be. We "name" them. Or, as Rebbe Nachman encouraged, we "help [them] return to G-d." Fred summed it up this way: "To be able to be accepted for who we are and to be able to grow from there is one of the great treasures of life."

We experienced this great treasure with our neighbor Junior. Having the grace to see the image of God in Junior allowed us to witness an even greater transformation: the image of God within him becoming conformed to the image of Christ.

After Junior prayed in the hospital with my husband for new life, he received it. On one of our visits to his home, he pulled my husband aside and told him that he knew a change had occurred in him because he was beginning to think differently. A fruit of that "thinking differently" was Junior's decision to go to neighbors with whom he had longstanding feuds—like the one between Jacob and Esau—and ask for forgiveness. He was looking through new eyes, eyes that recognized "what's wonderful" about his neighbor because they had recognized what was wonderful about himself. (This recognition of his self-worth even brought about some changes in his immediate environment, as he worked to cover up his dirt floors with cutout pieces of linoleum.)

My husband had talked to him about baptism, but Junior postponed the event because he hadn't been feeling well. But early on Easter morning he called Jeff and asked to be baptized that very day. When my husband asked about the change of heart and immediacy of the request, Junior said he had been reading the book of Acts and had seen the directive to be baptized there. Our church family witnessed his rebirth; we became *his* family, perhaps the first real family he ever had. But the sickness he felt on Christmas Day had presaged what the new year would bring. His health began to deteriorate. The diagnosis, long delayed, of bone cancer finally arrived. He was returned to the same hospital where my husband had first met him.

The hospital was located forty-five minutes away, and I tried to visit Junior as often as I could. My last memory of him was trying to give him a kiss good-bye and missing as I tried in vain to pull myself up over the bed rail. We both laughed. The next day, he didn't even remember I had been there. Then, late one Sunday night, Junior called my husband and asked him to come spend the night with him at the hospital. He didn't want to be alone. Jeff was understandably exhausted after a full day of services at the church, but he went and spent the night with Junior.

"It's the last thing I'll ever ask of you, Pastor," Junior said. And it was. He died two days later, just three weeks after his initial diagnosis. In one year's time, my husband had prayed with Junior for new life, baptized him, and performed his funeral. We, his adopted family, watched that new life flourish into new thoughts and new healings in relationships, become sealed in baptism, and culminate in reunion with Christ. At Junior's funeral, a friend of his gave us his Bible, the one we had given him for Christmas, along with three photographs of Junior. Two were black-and-white pictures from his school days. One was of him as an adult. Perhaps they comprised the whole of Junior's family photo album.

In *A Wind in the Door*, Meg asks the cherubim how someone is Named, and the angel answers: "Love. That's what makes persons know who they are."[6]

A few weeks after Junior's death, I was back in Pittsburgh for my second interview with Fred. It was a difficult time for both of us. He had just lost his longtime colleague and the *Neighborhood*'s musical director, jazz pianist Johnny Costa, to leukemia. Despite his grief, he had my own on his mind. I was waiting for him to complete some public service announcements, so I was sitting out of the way toward the entrance to the studio. I can't remember the exact topic of the piece he was taping, but it had to do with an appeal to help others in need.

"I was thinking of Junior just then, as I said those words," Fred shouted to me from across the studio during a pause in taping. He had just lost one of his dearest friends, but he was thinking of Junior.

"Is Junior your son?" a producer sitting near me asked, turning to look at me over her shoulder.

No, I thought to myself, *he's my neighbor*.

CHAPTER 6

THE POWER OF FORGIVENESS

Well, the older I get, man, the less I believe
in all those wonderful things I used to see
with those young eyes.
What could have happened?
So am I just growing up,
or is something else wrong?
Is the land of make-believe all gone?
Old King Friday just looks like a puppet, still.

Can you say jaded? or misunderstood?
Can you say hatred?
Sure, I knew you could. I knew you could.

From "Every Word You Said,"
Mark Robertson of This Train

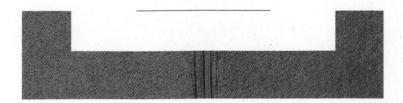

Seeing the best in ourselves so that we can see the best in our neighbor may sound like a utopian dream in a world that's "jaded," "misunderstood," and filled with "hatred." Perhaps that formula only works in the Neighborhood of Make-Believe, where the main characters, like King Friday, are controlled by higher-minded puppeteers. Real people, unfortunately, are under no such constraint. Certainly mischief enters the Neighborhood from time to time, as when in anger Lady Elaine Fairchild turns the Eiffel Tower upside down. But upside down is more the natural state of the larger world outside the WQED studio where the Neighborhood resides. Even if everyone in the Neighborhood bucks the trend by treating one another with respect, other television fare comes much closer to reflecting what awaits us in the real world.

Fred once told me he didn't watch much children's television, and when he did, it was usually what was sent to him: "I've seen some sample programs, and usually people who are producing children's programs send me what they consider is their *best* to see, so the samples that I see may be a little better than what is generally on the air each day." But he found out "what is generally on the air each day" when he stopped in to visit his grandsons on the way home from work one afternoon. The babysitter directed him upstairs, where his grandsons were watching television. As Fred entered the room he saw a popular superhero cartoon on the screen, with celluloid characters taking out their "neighbors" with machine guns.

I knew how Fred felt about guns; in fact, the only time I remember him taking legal action against a Mister Rogers parody was when a distributor sold T-shirts with a photo of him holding a handgun. The caption read, "Welcome to my 'hood." A kindly neighbor packing heat wasn't funny to Fred, nor was seeing his grandsons watch what was being passed off as children's television. These weren't cartoon animals brandishing anvils and frying pans but human characters solving their problems with deadly violence.

Fred sat down next to his youngest grandson, who was about five at the time, and confessed that what was happening on the screen was scary even to him, an adult. As the violence escalated, Fred commented again, this time interjecting that people shouldn't do that to one another. His grandson tried to allay Fred's fears by pointing out a plot element his grandfather might have missed: the targets of the machine guns were the bad guys.

Fred quickly countered that there are better ways to treat bad people than killing them. He said his grandson looked at him in bewilderment, as if that possibility had never been weighed in the avenging hero's scales of justice. The experience so unnerved Fred that before going to bed that night, he wrote a public service announcement for children and offered it to any station that would air it: "Some television programs are loud and scary, with people shooting and hitting each other. Well, you can do something about that. When you see scary television like that, you can turn it off. And when you do turn it off, that will show you that you are the strongest of them all. It takes a very strong person to be able to turn off scary TV."

A SOLUTION TO THE PROBLEM OF VIOLENCE

Fred's encouraging children to turn off scary TV was only the first step, in his mind. The next step was helping these same children (and their parents) to find appropriate ways to express their feelings, especially feelings of anger that can lead to the violence that scary TV often depicts. If you asked Fred for a psychological solution to the problem of violence, of hating your neighbor, he would sum it up in one word: *sublimation*.

A concept Fred likely learned in his graduate studies in child development, sublimation is the process by which socially unacceptable behaviors are channeled—sublimated —into more socially acceptable ways. The concept doesn't carry with it the idea that anger and violence can necessarily be eliminated, just that they can be diverted in ways that don't involve machine guns. Undesirable feelings or behaviors can be rerouted and released into excelling in sports or contributing to the arts, for example. From a very young age, Fred turned to the piano as a way to express his anger.

Fred told me that sublimation was the key to his song, "What Do You Do (with the Mad That You Feel?)." Through its lyrics he offers ways to redirect angry feelings: pounding clay, punching a bag, pounding dough, rounding up friends for a game of tag and running fast. "The world needs to learn to know what to do with negative feelings," he told me, explaining his motivation for writing the song. "It's so easy to pick up a gun and shoot somebody. It's so much healthier—and so much more dramatic—to work out something interpersonally with somebody and to come to a resolution that means weal in both people's life." And children weren't the only recipients of this message; Fred mentioned receiving mail from adults who told him that when they felt the urge to act out their anger in inappropriate ways, they remembered the words to his song and were able to stop themselves.

After her unacceptable paroxysm of anger in the Neighborhood of Make-Believe, Lady Elaine learned to pound and then mold clay as a way to manage her angry feelings. Fred wanted children from the earliest age (and their parents too) to know there is a way to redirect angry feelings away from our natural inclination to turn our worlds upside down.

ONE LITTLE WORD

And though this world, with devils filled,
should threaten to undo us,
we will not fear, for God hath willed
his truth to triumph through us.

The Prince of Darkness grim,
we tremble not for him;
his rage we can endure,
for lo, his doom is sure;
one little word shall fell him.

Martin Luther, "A Mighty Fortress Is Our God,"
translated by Frederick H. Hedge

Fred Rogers' spiritual answer to how we "treat bad people" is much more far-reaching than the psychology behind sublimation. And it's another lesson he learned from his beloved seminary professor, Dr. Orr, the lesson of Luther's "one little word."

Fred told me during our first meeting, "I'll never forget one time, and this was in [Dr. Orr's] latest years in the nursing home. Joanne and I used to visit him every Sunday in the nursing home." (A fellow seminary graduate once noted that Fred's faithful visits with Dr. Orr were typical of his "pastoral sensitivity.") "And we had just sung 'A

Mighty Fortress Is Our God' at the service, and I just wanted so much to ask him this question.

"I said, 'Dr. Orr, you know in that verse, it says something about—how does it go?—"The prince of darkness grim, we tremble not for him," and then it goes on, and then at the very end of that verse it says, "One little word shall fell him."'

"I said, 'Dr. Orr, what is that *one little word* that would wipe out the prince of darkness, fell him?'

"He thought for a moment, and said, 'Forgiveness. Father, forgive them for they know not what they do.' He said, 'You know, Fred, there is one thing that evil cannot stand, and that's forgiveness.' That's meant the world to me."

"And you've been able to pass that on to others," I offered.

He sighed deeply. "It's one of the toughest things in the world when somebody has hurt you, and you can find within yourself the strength to begin the whole process of forgiveness. And it turns out to be the gift to you, not so much the gift to the person you're forgiving."

"And that's the mercy of God, too . . ."

"Absolutely," he agreed, and his eyes filled with tears.

". . . that it reaches to both people."

It is possible to see the best in our neighbor because of one thing: forgiveness. It's possible to solve problems without machine guns because of one thing: forgiveness. That's not a concept unique to the Neighborhood of Make-Believe but to the kingdom of God.

Just hours before Fred's friend and colleague Johnny

Costa passed away, Fred went to visit him at the nursing home where he was being cared for. Fred talked to Johnny about the fact that we all need forgiveness, even if we are unaware of it. Then he took that opportunity to ask for Johnny's forgiveness for anything he might have done unintentionally to hurt his dear friend. That room in the nursing home, Fred later wrote to me, even recalling the room number (143), "seemed filled with the grace of forgiving love. I think everyone who was there sensed that grace—as well as the absence of all evil." Because there is one thing that evil cannot stand, and that's forgiveness.

LEGENDARY FORGIVENESS

I'm sure you don't have much time,
but heroes are hard to find
Would you be mine? Could you be mine?

Mark Robertson, "Every Word You Said"

Sometimes the harm done to our neighbor is not of a physical kind, but the pain can be just as great—or greater.

When a woman meeting Fred for the first time likened her encounter to a religious experience, I knew what she was talking about. Fred did have that aura about him, as if peacefulness spun itself around him like a silk-stranded cocoon and seeped out through the fibers to those around him. It wasn't just the awe of celebrity that moved you; celebrity usually exudes entitlement more than it does peace.

Only once before in my life had I met someone with that kind of presence. I was twelve years old at the time, and it was during my confirmation. I was raised in the Catholic church (my first career goal was to become a nun, but marrying a Protestant minister ruffled those plans), and at the time of my confirmation, Joseph Bernardin was the archbishop of Cincinnati. (He later became a cardinal and served as prelate in Chicago.) He officiated at my confirmation, and when it came my turn to receive Communion, I remember looking into his eyes and knowing for the first time in my life that I had seen the face of Christ in another. His eyes expressed a warmth and compassion I had never before felt from another person, and they reached deep into my young soul. I never forgot that.

Years later, reading Cardinal Bernardin's book of personal reflections, *The Gift of Peace,* I found that others had had "religious experiences" around him as well. And that was his intention:

> I tried to look everyone in the eye and make each person feel that he or she was important, the only one present at the moment. . . . When you convince people that you really care and that, even if hundreds of others are around, at that particular moment they are the only ones that count—then you establish a new relationship. . . . You have

somehow mediated the love, mercy, and compassion of the Lord. In other words, the encounter also has a significant religious dimension: It helps strengthen the bond, the relationship, between each person and God.[1]

In 1996, many, many years after my confirmation, I wrote Cardinal Bernardin a letter, requesting a television interview. I had been reading about his new ministry to those who shared the burden of cancer with him (he was diagnosed with pancreatic cancer in 1995) and his new-found calling as the "unofficial chaplain" to cancer patients. I also knew he was one of those rare individuals who, like Fred and like Dr. Orr, knew and communicated the truth. The Cardinal graciously accepted my invitation, and we planned to do the interview after his upcoming spinal surgery. I wrote to Fred about the impending interview.

His reply was swift, as always: "*How wonderful that you will be interviewing Cardinal Bernardin! He has been such a hero to so many. His forgiveness of his accuser is legendary and healing: a real reflection of Jesus. I often think of what my professor-friend Dr. Orr used to say: 'The only thing that evil cannot stand is forgiveness.' That, of course, includes self and others. You can be assured of my prayers for the Cardinal and you.*"

His forgiveness of his accuser. Cardinal Bernardin's struggle with cancer had not been his only hardship in recent years. The cancer was preceded by another assault: the accusation that he had sexually abused a young seminarian many years before. In a torrent of church scandal and legitimate sexual abuse allegations, Cardinal Bernardin stood falsely accused. His accuser was Steven Cook, formerly a college student at Saint Gregory's Seminary in Cincinnati, where the abuse was alleged to have happened.

After one hundred days of conjecture, legal missteps, and name-smearing, the accusation was finally proven false, but the damage had been done. The second blow came a year later when Cardinal Bernardin was diagnosed with pancreatic cancer. A few days after his diagnosis, as the Cardinal was entering Loyola University Cancer Center to have surgery, a reporter stopped him and asked, "Which did you find more difficult or more traumatic—the false accusation or the diagnosis of cancer?"

The Cardinal immediately answered, "The false accusation." When asked for an explanation, he replied, "I told them that that the accusation had been the result of evil. It was an attack on my integrity, which, had it prevailed, would have ruined my credibility, my ability to lead. But cancer is an illness. It doesn't involve moral evil."[2]

Cardinal Bernardin must have also known the one thing that evil cannot stand; he chose to forgive his accuser. He met with Steven Cook, who died from AIDS nine months later, reconciling with him through forgiveness and the sacrament of Communion. I'm sure the face of Christ that I saw in Joseph Bernardin when he served me Communion at my confirmation was the same face reflected to Steven.

"For to see your face is like seeing the face of God," Jacob had said to Esau upon their reconciliation (Genesis 33:10).

The Cardinal wrote of his encounter with Steven: "As we flew back to Chicago that evening . . . I felt the lightness of spirit that an afternoon of grace brings to one's life. I could not help but think that the ordeal of the accusation led straight to this extraordinary experience of God's grace. . . . And I could not help but recall the work of the Good Shepherd: to seek and restore to the sheepfold the one that has been, only for a while, lost."[3]

After his initial surgery, Cardinal Bernardin was cancer free for fifteen months. The cancer returned at the end of August 1996, this time in his liver. His back surgery, the one after which I was to interview him, was canceled, and with the cancer's return, so was our interview. When he died three months later, he was ready. Part of his preparation had been a visit from Fred's dear friend Henri Nouwen, who visited the Cardinal and counseled him to look upon death as a friend, as a transition from this life to eternal life. The Cardinal never suspected that this "transition" would occur for Henri before himself; Henri died suddenly of a heart attack a short time later.

The Cardinal died on November 14, 1996, just thirteen days after completing *The Gift of Peace*. Fred called me from his home as soon as he heard the news. Together we talked about grief and the legacy that those who go before us leave behind. For the Cardinal, it was his singular expression of the power of forgiveness.

TOAST STICKS FOR THE EYES

'Cause I believed every word you said,
Mister Rogers, or can I call you Fred?
Mister Rogers, I could use a friend.
Mister Rogers, have we reached the end?

Mark Robertson, "Every Word You Said"

In his tribute to Mister Rogers, scattered throughout this chapter, recording artist Mark Robertson points out the discrepancy between the "beautiful days" in Mister Rogers' Neighborhood and the stark reality of a hate-filled and jaded world. But he doesn't dismiss the *possibility* of Mister Rogers' ideals; he still wants to believe every word Mister Rogers said. He echoes the sentiment of many disillusioned by life: "Mister Rogers, I could use a friend."

It isn't that Mister Rogers presented one side of reality and not the other; he wasn't unaware of the chaos and confusion in the world (and that they were sometimes fed to children through the airwaves). He appreciated and represented the intricacies of life and showed an appreciation for complex and conflicting feelings. He wasn't naïve; he knew that seeing the best in ourselves so that we can see the best in our neighbor—an act that translates into harmonious relationships—is only possible because of forgiveness.

In his moving parable, *Old Turtle and the Broken Truth*, Douglas Wood describes what happens when a truth falls from the stars. The truth breaks into pieces when it lands, and those who find it see that written on it are the words, "You are loved." The discoverers cherish the broken truth, never realizing that a half-truth can be dangerous. The people begin to fear those who don't share their truth, and those who covet the truth wage war against those who possess it. Finally Old Turtle reveals to a young seeker the missing part of the broken truth: "You are loved . . . and so are they." God's love is not only for us but also for our neighbors, and that's what allows us to cultivate the toast sticks for the eyes: encouraging others to be their honest selves, being a good neighbor, and offering forgiveness.

III.

TOAST STICKS FOR THE HANDS

CHAPTER 7

———————

THE LEAST OF THESE

———————

I have friends whom this world might call minimal as far
as not only their station in life, but their level of
intelligence and buying power. These friends to me
have been some of the greatest blessings that
I've known.

FRED, DURING ONE OF MY VISITS TO THE NEIGHBORHOOD

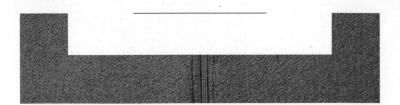

One Sunday morning in early spring my family arrived at church to find new faces assembled up front, an ensemble invited to provide special music for the morning's service. It wasn't a choir of children with freshly combed hair and too-big smiles or a celebrity singer with his own tour bus (and a too-perfect smile); it was a group of grown men and women with mental and physical disabilities. Some were blind, some had hearing aids, and all had severe mental disabilities. They comprised a bell choir, and their brightly colored bells, against the backdrop of their black-and-white attire, were not "just for decoration" (as are, I tell my kids, our bathroom guest towels). The colors corresponded to the color-coded cards the choir director held. As the music started for "Amazing Grace," the director held up the cards so the choir members knew when to ring their bells—a bell choir by flashcards. One short man in the back row shook his instrument so vigorously I thought the tongue of the bell would dislodge and go flying. I had to look away when his color came up—burgundy— because his unbridled enthusiasm in the face of his difficulties pricked my heart and made me cry.

The second song was "Were You There When They Crucified My Lord?" and during the final verse, we all stood together and sang:

> *Were you there when He rose up from the grave?*
> *Were you there when He rose up from the grave?*
> *Were you there when He rose up from the grave?*
> *Oh! Sometimes it causes me to tremble, tremble.*
> [Only two trembles, the director had warned us,
> or we won't finish all together!]
> *Were you there when He rose up from the grave?*

The solo performer was next. With eyes closed, he had to be led onstage. He groped about for the microphone, which the director put in his hand as a signal to begin. "Our Father," he sang a cappella, beginning with fits and starts. "Give," he sang and then tried again in another key: "Gi—" and then "Give, give us this day." A child up front snickered. Other times his voice sounded clear and beautiful, almost celestial. "For Thine is the kingdom and the power," he sang with great self-possession, but "and the glory" came out as a screech. It was this unevenness in his performance that made him such a contradiction, and such an inspiration. Everyone stood and clapped, and the director remembered that the first time this had happened, the singer remarked on the way home, "I got a standing ovation." Then he had paused and asked, "What is a standing ovation?"

After the service, I went up front to thank the choir and to shake their hands. One woman would have none of that and threw her arms around my neck in a near strangle. "Hi! How are you? Hi. How are you doing?" she said over and over and held on tighter.

They needed color-coded cards to serve God, but they did it with a purity of intent and an innocence (and for one man, an enthusiasm) that both inspired and shamed me. Jesus may have had these dedicated servants in mind when He said, "Let the little children come to me, and do not hinder them, for the kingdom of God belongs to such as these" (Mark 10:14).

Of course the members of the bell choir weren't children in the literal sense, but according to Fred, they didn't need to be.

"Let the little ones come to me and forbid them not," he told me, repeating Jesus' words, "because, boy, the kingdom of heaven is filled with little people, and that doesn't mean in size. That means people who are disenfranchised and know that they need God—that's who teaches us."

AN ADVOCATE FOR "SUCH AS THESE"

Fred was a lifelong student of those Jesus called "such as these," but he was also their advocate. From the start, he was a champion of those who demonstrated a special vulnerability, especially children. Fred's advocacy began early in his career, out of necessity. One of the most moving moments of his memorial service (in May 2003) was a tape of Fred's appearance before the U.S. Senate Subcommittee on Communications in 1969, when a twenty-million-dollar grant for public television was hanging in the balance.

Mister Rogers was little known then because his program had just begun airing nationally the year before. He would appear before Senator John Pastore, a Democrat from Rhode Island who, in addition to his distinction as the first Italian American elected to the U.S. Senate, was also well known for his brusque and unyielding nature.

Enter a young Fred Rogers with slick black hair and a tidy suit, not yet an American icon.

"Senator Pastore, this is a philosophical statement," Fred said, pointing to a text copy of the essay he had submitted, "and would take about ten minutes to read, so I'll not do that." His voice reflected the slow and measured cadence that would soon become synonymous with his name, just the sort of characteristic that would have annoyed a man like Senator Pastore. "One of the first things that a child learns in a healthy family is trust, and I *trust* what you've said, that you'll read this. It's very important to me; I care deeply about children, my first—"

Senator Pastore didn't wait for Fred to finish: "Will it make you happy if you read it?" Even without seeing the footage, you can hear the condescension in his voice.

"I'd—just like to talk about it, if it's all right—"

Senator Pastore cut him off again with a brisk, "Fine."

"This is what I give," Fred continued. "I give an expression of care every day to each child, to help him realize that he is unique. I end the program by saying, 'You've made this day a special day by just your being you. There's no person in the whole world like you, and I like you just the way you are.' I feel that if we in public television can only make it clear that feelings are mentionable and manageable, we will have done a great service."

After a long pause, Senator Pastore responded, "I'm supposed to be a pretty tough guy. This is the first time I've had goose bumps in the last two days."

"Well, I'm grateful," Fred answered calmly and sincerely, "not only for your goose bumps but for your interest in our kind of communication." (Fred's gratitude for the senator's goose bumps drew much laughter from the crowd watching the tape at the memorial service, but Fred wasn't trying to be funny. His face remained steely and resolute; he knew that parting the Red Sea is not the same as walking through it.)

Fred then recited with great conviction the words to his song, "What Do You Do (with the Mad That You Feel)?" Watching the footage, you get a sense that what he was doing at the time was taking his own mad—his anger at the tenuous nature of public television at the time—and channeling it into an impassioned plea for the little people he knew comprised the kingdom of God: the helpless, the impressionable, the guileless, those for whom television can be either an advocate or an accuser; those who through television will see either what is good about them or what is bad about them. Maybe even those who would be offered in its place, should public television fail, avenging super-heroes who were lauded for killing off the bad guys.

Fred concluded the song with the lyric, "[You can] know that there's something deep inside that helps us become what we can."

Visibly moved, Senator Pastore, no longer inclined to interrupt, said, "I think it's wonderful. That is just so wonderful. Looks like you just won the twenty million dollars."

The people at Fred's memorial service, viewing the foot-age nearly thirty-four years to the day later, had the same response as those at the original hearing: spontaneous, joyous applause. We weren't applauding a simple David and Goliath victory, although most people enjoy seeing the underdog triumph over the giant. Instead, we were rejoicing in the collective realization that what is better than conquest is convert—and Fred Rogers had just won himself one.

BECOMING LIKE LITTLE CHILDREN

The child is in me still . . . and sometimes not so still.

Fred Rogers

When Jesus told His followers, "Unless you change and become like little children, you will never enter the kingdom of heaven" (Matthew 18:3), He was pointing toward the vulnerability and openness that are essential for those of us who aren't children to inherit the kingdom of God. This identification with children was important to Fred.

"I just love hearing from those people who watched the *Neighborhood* when they were children and are now adults. And many of them [are] parents themselves. And they say, 'I sit and watch with my child and remember what it was like for me to be a child.' Well, that is a service that the [program] really gives to people because *if parents can remember what it was like to be a child, they are going to be much more empathic with their own children.*"

Fred learned this empathy from many people but especially from his maternal grandfather, Fred McFeely, for whom Fred (whose full name is Fred McFeely Rogers) was named. His grandfather not only became the namesake for the Speedy Delivery man in the Neighborhood (Mr. McFeely), but he also bequeathed something to his grandson that Fred would pass on to his television neighbors in nearly all of the nine hundred episodes of *Mister Rogers' Neighborhood.*

Fred told me about a particular afternoon he spent with his grandfather and the legacy he passed on to him. "Whenever we would visit my grandfather on his farm— he had some stone walls—and I would love to walk on those walls. My mother and my grandmother were very protective of me, and they would say, 'Freddy, be careful! You might fall!' And my grandfather would say [Fred imitated his grandfather's gruff voice], 'Let the kid walk on the wall; he's got to learn to do things for himself.'

"Here was somebody who was supporting my individuation, you know."

(*Individuation*, like *sublimation*, was a term Fred probably acquired in his graduate studies in child development. The Jungian term refers to a lifelong process of integrating influences and instincts that make a person whole, a discovery of his or her uniqueness. It also carries with it the idea that we become who we were intended to be, by design, not just who we think we should be. Fred's longtime colleague and associate producer Hedda Sharapan once compared *Mister Rogers' Neighborhood* to a child development textbook, translated by Fred.)

"[My grandfather was] supporting the things that I was trying out. It's great to have people like that in your life, and I hope that, well, as a matter of fact, he was the one who said, 'You've made this day a special day by just your being you, Freddy.' [The very words he introduced to Senator Pastore many years later.] That saying is up on the wall in my office; a friend had that made for me. It says, 'Freddy, you've made this day a special day by just your being you.' Well, I've been able to pass that on to other children."

And if there is one thing that viewers remember about Mister Rogers, even as adults, it's the sense of acceptance

in his assertion that you are special "by just your being you."

"Are you that kind of grandfather to Alexander and Douglas?" I asked.

"Oh, I hope so. Oh, but I'm so blessed to have them. I mean, here's another chance to grow. I felt that with Jay [Jamie] and John, our sons. This was a chance for me to live again all those developmental tasks that I went through at their age. *And if you can be open to that, you blossom.*"

THE HELPERS

Becoming like children, like the "little people" Fred referred to, involves more than just identification. There is a reciprocal relationship between the disenfranchised, those who know they need God, and others. They teach us as we help them. For Fred, this practical outworking of loving our neighbor—using not only our heart and eyes but our hands—is what defined a hero: "To see people who will notice a need in the world and do something about it, and rather than view it with despair they view it with hope—that to me is such an enormous gift in this life. Those are my heroes.

"You know, there are so many people who say, 'It's not my kid, it's not my school, it's not my community'—you know, 'forget it.' But there are some others who say, 'It is my kid, it is my school . . .'"

Fred's mother had always called these people "the helpers." When he was a boy and he was frightened by some news

he had heard, his mother would say, "Look for the helpers. You will always find people who are helping." Fred did look for the helpers, those who notice a need in the world and do something about it, and they became his heroes, modeling the lesson Jesus taught His disciples, as recorded in Matthew 25:35–45.

Helpers are people like Dr. Orr, who not only taught theology but also lived it. Fred remembered one day when Dr. Orr went out to lunch on a winter afternoon and came back without his overcoat. Fred asked him about his errant coat, and Dr. Orr simply replied that he had another one at home. He never let on that he had given it to someone who didn't have one.

"I needed clothes and you clothed me."

Another helper was Henri Nouwen, the prolific writer who taught at Harvard but resigned to become pastor to the disabled members of the L'Arche community in Toronto. Among Henri's daily responsibilities was the bathing, shaving, dressing, and feeding of a severely disabled man named Adam. In the end, Henri noted, it was Adam who taught *him*. This is why Fred called Henri "one of my revered people in this life; he's a hero."

"I was sick and you looked after me."

Helper William Wasson started a ministry for "Our Little Brothers and Sisters" in Mexico. Fred told me why he considered Father Wasson his hero: "He went to Mexico forty years ago to die. He was very ill. Obviously he didn't die. He was in a little parish there, and there were two kids who

were stealing from the church's poor box, and those kids were taken to jail. And Bill Wasson went to the jail and said, 'Do you think I could take care of those kids at home?' and they said, 'Sure,' you know, 'gladly.' So he took them home, and two days later the people at the jail called and said, 'We've got two more,' and he said, 'Send them over.' Well, in a matter of a month he had about seventeen kids, and he had to move to bigger quarters, and he's adopted them all, legally adopted all these kids.

"In the last twenty-five years he has adopted about six thousand children. They have their own schools, and many of them now are second generation, and they have come back to help work with the new pequeños who are coming. They have places in Haiti; I went to visit a place in Haiti that they have for babies with AIDS." Father Wasson went to Mexico to die but instead discovered a reason to live.

"I was a stranger and you invited me in."

Fred was a helper too. He didn't view the television set as a protective buffer between himself and his audience, like the raised pulpit of old that elevated the preacher above the common fray. He wasn't afraid to get his hands dirty. He once told me he went into a maximum-security prison in Pittsburgh and taught a college course in child development. "I'm still in touch with a couple of the students (one was released, one was not)," he wrote in a letter. I noticed that he used the word "students" and not "inmates." He was their teacher, but in return he learned from them and forged enduring friendships.

"I was in prison and you came to visit me."

"Lord, when did we see you hungry and feed you, or thirsty and give you something to drink?" the disciples asked Him. "When did we see you a stranger and invite you in, or needing clothes and clothe you? When did we see you sick or in prison and go to visit you?"

Jesus replied, "I tell you the truth, whatever you did for one of the least of these brothers of mine, you did for me" (see Matthew 25:35–40).

A PIVOTAL MOMENT OF POTENTIAL

Fred once referred to himself as an "emotional archaeologist," always looking for the root of things, and I share with him this desire to find out what motivates people, what propels them to make choices that affect their lives and the lives of others.

He had always told me he got into television because he saw people throwing pies in each other's faces, and he deplored such demeaning behavior. But knowing the depth of Fred Rogers, I knew there had to be more to the story, if I just dug a little deeper. What was the impetus to his lifelong commitment to the "least of these"? An archeologist knows to go back to the beginning of things.

What most people don't know about Fred Rogers is that, as a child, he was scared to death to go to school. It's hard to conceive that someone who was so respectful and caring in both his public and private life was the victim of bullying; but as a shy, overweight eight-year-old, Freddy Rogers was a prime target for schoolyard bullies. That's why he was usually driven to and from school each day. But one day, when the students were released early, Freddy started to walk home by himself. A passel of boys followed. After looking over his shoulder, he began to walk faster. So did they. Soon they were closing in, shouting, "Hey, Fat Freddy!" and threatening, "We're going to get you, Fat Freddy!"

Little Fred Rogers ran and ran and ran. He knew if he could get to the home of a family friend, a widow named Mrs. Stewart, who lived nearby, he could find refuge. While the bullies kept taunting, he silently prayed that she would be home. He banged on the door, and Mrs. Stewart swung it open to let him in. The bullies took their defeat and went on their way.

Well-meaning adults told him to shrug off the incident. "Just let on that you don't care," they suggested. "Then nobody will bother you."

But even as a child, Fred Rogers knew that wasn't the answer: "I resented the teasing. I resented the pain. I resented those kids for not seeing beyond my fatness or my shyness." He wanted someone to tell him it was okay to feel that way, it was okay to feel bad about what happened, and even to feel sad (a gift he would later give to my son). "I cried to myself whenever I was alone," he told me. "I cried through my fingers as I made up songs on the piano. I sought out stories of other people who were poor in spirit, and I felt for them."

It was a pivotal moment in his childhood, a moment with the potential to turn him irreparably inward—or worse, into a bully himself. Instead it set him searching: "I started to look behind the things that people did and said and . . . after a lot of sadness, I began a lifelong search for what is essential, what it is about my neighbor that doesn't meet the eye." He noticed a need in the world and chose to do something about it; rather than view it with despair, he viewed it with hope.

But something more had happened. Little Fred Rogers learned—in the most tangible way possible—that God can be depended upon, that He is *always* there: "The tough times I've been through . . . turned out to be times in which God's presence was so clear—so real that it felt like Mrs. Stewart opening her door and taking me into her safe home."

Out of his deep hurt came a longing to soothe the pain of others, and out of the callous disregard of schoolyard bullies came a determination to only lift up—and never demean—his neighbor. Out of God's provision for him through a loving widow came his assurance of the omnipresence of a living God.

At last I had it: Fred's intense devotion to the disenfranchised, to the least of these, arose from the realization that he was one of them.

CHAPTER 8

———————————

DIFFICULT TIMES

———————————

The story has been floating around for years and has had several incarnations, although the response to the story is remarkably consistent. The account goes something like this: Fred Rogers' car is stolen. A few days later the car is returned to the exact spot from where it was stolen, along with this note: "We're sorry. We didn't know it was *your* car."

Sometimes the thieves find a script for *Mister Rogers' Neighborhood* in the back seat or a stray Daniel Striped Tiger puppet in the trunk or hear on the news that it was Mister Rogers' car. In some variations they clean and vacuum the car before returning it, and in other versions they just leave a note (either on the dash or under the wiper). One Pittsburgh native's account includes the added drama that the thieves had already begun dismantling the car when they discovered who it belonged to. They quickly reassembled the car and deposited it in Fred's driveway— same-day service—with a handwritten note of apology.

The details vary, but not the response. "Is there a single other human being in history who could inspire such an act?" people remark upon hearing the story. "Who else could make criminals behave like *that*?"

I've never bothered to find out whether this story is true or the stuff of urban legend. Other stories being circulated, like the one that Fred's sweaters hid a tattooed upper body or that he served as a sniper in the military, are easily discounted (several episodes of the *Neighborhood* show Fred swimming with no sign of a single tattoo on his body, and it's impossible to enlist in the military when you have flunked the physical). But the penitent-thieves story has become part of the Mister Rogers lore (just as the never-uttered catchphrase, "Can you say _____?" has), and veracity doesn't seem to be as important to most people as believability. No one questions the story's believability because if anyone *could* make criminals behave, it would have been Mister Rogers.

This story contains the nucleus of another of Mister Rogers' powerful life lessons: how we see others affects how we treat others. What people saw in Fred Rogers made them want to be better people, an extension of Madeleine L'Engle's concept of "Naming" in *A Wind in the Door*: "You're supposed to make earthlings feel more human," the cherubim tells the novel's young heroine.

To make others feel more human, Fred sought to see their Maker in them and then to treat them accordingly. This is one reason why he had so much respect for the custom of bowing, more distinctive to other cultures than to our own. Bowing to one another shows appreciation, Fred would say, especially for what is "eternal" within the other. The inner disciplines of taking time and of prayer, directed by the Holy Spirit, affect how we see others. To fully see others, we need to recognize who we are as individuals, love our neighbor as ourselves, and forgive often. The practical outworking of these toast sticks for the heart and eyes are accomplished through the hands.

When a Web designer made a popular parody of *Mister Rogers' Neighborhood* and posted it online, he knew he was protected by copyright law (he was an attorney, after all). He offered to voluntarily remove it, out of "respect and affection" for Mister Rogers, if he found out that Fred didn't like it. When the Web designer/attorney learned that was the case, he took the site down, despite its popularity. Of his decision he wrote, "I do genuinely esteem Fred Rogers (whose television Neighborhood I visited for countless hours when I was a young boy). So, I took the site down. *In my interior, psychic battle between the macho lawyer persona and the demands of the Sermon on the Mount, the latter won. And I suppose that Fred's gentle, formative influence might have had something to do with that.*"[1]

While most of us would marvel at that kind of respect—from both those who break the law (like car thieves) and those who concede in spite of their legal rights (like this attorney)—Fred believed we are all worthy of that respect. He also believed we should show that kind of respect to others and that such treatment should be the rule (the Golden Rule, in fact), not the exception.

THE NATURE OF LOSS

We live life as if it were a motion picture. Loss turns life into a snapshot. The movement stops; everything freezes.

Gerald Sittser, *A Grace Disguised*

When Jesus set forth the Golden Rule (changing a popular religious proverb from "do not do unto others what you would not want them to do unto you" into a proactive stance), He was highlighting the fact that there is more to the spiritual life than just inner disciplines and rightly seeing our neighbor as being made in the image of God. It is as though He saw the negative turn of the proverb—"do not do unto others"—as too passive. In contrast, "Do unto others" is a command to act.

One of the principle ways Fred implemented Jesus' command was to acknowledge the pain and suffering of his neighbor and then to act upon that awareness by reaching out and offering comfort. "I've had losses; everybody has had losses," he once told me, making clear that while loss in life is the great equalizer, it also opens doors for us to connect with others.

"I've had friends who have had deep trouble, as far as mourning is concerned, and to be able to participate in the life of someone who is in deep grief has been a great gift too. Jesus said, 'Blessed are they who mourn.' He didn't say, 'Blessed are the people who comfort them that mourn.' He said, 'Blessed are they that mourn.' [They that mourn] definitely give gifts to those with whom they choose to be in their mourning. And they also give gifts to themselves.

"Someone who is in deep grief and can allow God to dwell in the deepest recesses of their lives can come through that experience as a far more mature, far more blessed person. I would never wish a catastrophe on anybody, but I have over and over seen the grace that can come from horrendous experiences in life." (As an example of such grace, Fred pointed toward one of his television neighbors, John Secora, with whom he had been taping a program that day. John, who came to the Neighborhood to teach Fred exercises, had been in a car accident that had left him paralyzed from the waist down. But John was determined to continue his affinity for sports from his wheelchair. "I just find being in his presence a wonderful thing," Fred told me.)

In order to comfort others, to participate in the life of someone who is in deep grief, we need to know what it feels like to experience loss ourselves. When I asked Fred about loss in his own life, he briefly talked about the loneliness of his childhood. Then he quickly turned to a story from his son's childhood.

"I'll never forget the time that Joanne and I had Jamie, that's our older son, at the beach, and he had suntan lotion on him, and he was dropped in the water, and we lost him.

And I was frantic, and of course Joanne was too. I'll never forget—we thought, *Well, we'll just have to go get an ambulance or something.* We didn't know what to do."

"Loss turns life into a snapshot. The movement stops; everything freezes."

"I just said, 'Dear God, help us find him!' I just screamed it out.

"And it wasn't a matter of ten seconds that I saw this little foot in the water, and I grabbed for the foot, and it was so slippery that he went under again. Salt water is very difficult to find kids in, but eventually I got him. And the three of us just sat on the beach, and I'll never forget his cry because then I knew that he was alive, and of course all the water came out and so forth. But that cry was one, well, it was the second happiest cry that we had had because the first was when he was born. . . .

"It was as if he was given to us a second time."

While it was obvious from Fred's breathless telling of the story that Jamie's near-drowning still evoked strong emotion, in the end what he lost was given back to him. The circumstances, though traumatic, were reversible and mendable, like a broken arm.

Other types of loss are less kind, less predictable, less willing to give back. Author and religion professor Gerald Sittser wrote in his powerful treatise on grief, *A Grace Disguised*, that if reversible loss is like a broken arm, then catastrophic loss is more like an amputated limb. Sittser didn't draw his conclusion from aloft an ivory tower but from deep in the trenches of personal tragedy. His wife, his mother, and his young daughter were taken from him in a single car accident, and the drunk driver responsible for the accident walked away unpunished.

"All people suffer loss," he wrote, echoing Fred's sentiments. "Being alive means suffering loss." But some loss is unrecoverable, and participants in that kind of loss walk around with part of themselves missing. Their lives are truncated, and as an added cruelty, phantom pains continue to haunt. Nerves prickle the memory of what is no longer there.

THE GIFT OF
ALLOWING OTHERS TO GRIEVE

Fred experienced losses like this too, losses that couldn't be reversed or recovered as easily as stolen cars that magically reappear in the driveway. One loss I have already written about, the death of his longtime friend and music director, Johnny Costa. Fred told me of Johnny's death in a letter: "*Johnny Costa died last Friday. We start in the studio without him next week. I'd be very grateful for your prayers.*"

Johnny had been a part of the *Neighborhood* and Fred's friend for three decades, and his death made Fred feel as if part of himself were missing; so much so (I found out years later) that Fred considered shutting down production of *Mister Rogers' Neighborhood* permanently after Johnny's death. When I called Fred to tell him how sorry I was about

Johnny's death, he told me how difficult it would be to go into work the next day, the first day in nearly thirty years that production would start without Johnny.

"But, tomorrow, when I go in the studio," he said slowly and deliberately, "I'm going to look over to the right side of the studio where you and I last sat together, and I'll think of you and draw strength from the fact that you're praying for me." Fred wasn't only willing to offer comfort; he was willing to receive it.

Just as he heralded the importance of expressing other kinds of emotions, Fred felt it essential to give others permission to grieve over the losses in their lives. He learned that lesson himself when he was six years old.

"I'll never forget when my Granddad Rogers died. I found my own father on the second floor of their house—crying," he told me during one of our interviews. "This [was] when Granddad Rogers was lying in state, and people were coming to visit, and years later when my own father died, I remembered that time so vividly. I thought, *Dad cried when his dad died*. That certainly gave me broad license to cry when he died. And my sons saw me, and so when I die, I trust that they'll know that it's okay to cry too."

And of course they did.

"You know, that's a gift that can be passed on for generations," he added, "the gift of knowing that it's all right to express how you're feeling."

Sometimes, without even knowing it, we give permission to others to express their feelings. For several years

while my husband was pastoring, I took his place in the pulpit to speak on Mother's Day. It might not seem like much of a Mother's Day gift to have to prepare a message and work through the jitters of speaking to a congregation, but I thought of it this way: at least it got me out of the nursery, where my husband took *my* place.

But during one Mother's Day service, toward the end of the message, I felt overcome by emotion and could not finish the sermon. I tried, but only tears came out. I wrote to Fred about the experience (he may have recalled that the same thing had happened to me once when I was praying for him). He replied, "*Thank you for your generous letter. I've been thinking of you and Jeff, Jonathan and Emily so much. . . . You can be sure that your Mother's Day sermon will always be remembered. You gave everyone the permission to be sad about losses in their lives (Mother's Day often evokes such losses anyway) AND you let the congregation know how deeply you cared about them and your time with them. Your recounting the story of your Mother's Day sermon (and your not "finishing" it) reminded me of one of my favorite quotations from St. Francis of Assisi: 'Preach the Gospel at all times, when necessary use words.' . . . I'm grateful for our friendship.*"

Fred was especially concerned about offering this permission to grieve to children. Once when I asked him a question on behalf of a little boy who was sad over his parents' separation, Fred replied directly to the boy, "I think one of the toughest things for children is for their parents

not to be getting along, and so divorce feels like it's just ripping a piece of cloth apart, and for children to try to understand that is sometimes way beyond their capacities. So you really need somebody to help you know that both your mother and your dad love you. It wasn't your fault that your mom and dad don't live together, and it won't be your fault if they get a divorce. As a matter of fact, you are probably one of the best things that has ever happened to your mom and your dad. And they'll love you as long as they live—and even longer.

"But for a little child to have a mom and dad that don't like each other, it's very important for you to know that they still love you."

Fred wanted to make sure this little boy knew that his parents' problems weren't his fault and that they still loved him. But he also acknowledged the boy's very real loss: divorce feels like ripping a piece of cloth apart. He didn't treat it as if it were a broken arm but as the dramatic and irrevocable loss that it was.

IN LOSS, AN OVERSHADOWING PRESENCE

When your heart can cry another's sadness,
Then your heart is full of love.

Josie Carey Franz and Fred Rogers,
"Then Your Heart Is Full of Love"

One of the idiosyncrasies of Fred's letter-writing that especially endeared me to him was his habit of always adding a little something extra. This was true for my children as well. When my daughter's track record at the dentist was greatly improved by my reading Fred's book *Going to the Dentist* to her, he sent her an autographed copy. (And when I say "greatly improved," I mean the dentist made it through the entire appointment without experiencing her knee reflex.) So that my son wouldn't feel left out, Fred sent along an autographed copy of his book *Making Friends* for him.

In his letters to me he would often send photocopies of quotes that he found in books (like the one by Gerald May I mentioned back in chapter 3) or articles he wanted me to read. "*Dear Amy, Reading this—especially the many expressions of 'creativity'—reminded me of you!*" he wrote at the top of a column by author Ron Rolheiser that he had copied and slipped into the envelope with his letter.

Once he saw a young boy featured on a magazine cover that he thought looked like my son, so he photocopied it and sent it with a note asking whether it was. (It wasn't, but the effort he took to find out for sure always astounded me.) When I told him I was learning to play the piano, he wrote out the notes, on his own carefully rendered staff, to "Jubilate Deo," his morning exclamation of praise.

Many times he would write messages on the back of the envelopes, as if the paper inside wasn't fully able to hold the contents of the letter and they teemed over onto the outsides. Or perhaps a thought occurred to him after he had already sealed the envelope. "*How grateful we are for your loving prayers!*" he once wrote, above the squiggle of his initials. Another time he added this question: "*Do you know the sermons of Fred B. Craddock? I've been reading one collection,* The Cherry Log Sermons, *which is SUPERB!! (I'd love to order it for you if you don't have it.) F.*"

I looked forward to these little add-ons as much as the letters inside. But none struck me as profoundly as this lengthy note, not Fred's own words this time, but a quote he had copied and carefully taped to the outside of the envelope: "Life is so generous a giver, but we, judging its gifts by their covering, cast them away as ugly or heavy or hard. Remove the covering and you will find beneath it a living splendor, woven of love, by wisdom, with power. Welcome it, grasp it, and you touch the angel's hand that brings it to you. Everything we call a trial, a sorrow, or a duty, believe me, that angel's hand is there; the gift is there, and the wonder of an overshadowing presence."

The words were penned by Fra Giovanni, a sixteenth-century priest and scholar, in his letter to a countess ("I am your friend and my love for you goes deep," the letter, written on Christmas Eve 1513, begins). It's fitting that these words, these penetrating observations, were originally written in a letter, from one friend in his attempt to encourage another. Fred never referred to the quote in his letter, but I knew he was trying to remind me of something: there is an "overshadowing presence" in all loss.

I needed that reminder; for many months I had felt very much alone, perhaps even abandoned. I've read that one of the most difficult things about suffering is the apparent aimlessness of it all, and I would add to that, loneliness. I was most lonely for God, for a sense of His overshadowing presence.

It started innocuously enough, with a twinge of pain in my pelvic area that I noticed around Christmastime and attributed to the stress of the holidays. After the new year began, the pain became debilitating. I had exploratory surgery, as my doctor thought the pain was caused by endometriosis. The surgery showed nothing, and I was sent to another specialist (and two more after that). In between I got an ambulance ride to the emergency room when my blood-sugar level dropped so low I couldn't move, not even to wipe the tears from my eyes.

Then one day while I was confined to bed because of the pain, still without diagnosis, my son, who was four at the time, came to me and reported, "Emily coughed, and now she is taking a nap." The "nap" turned out to be unconsciousness from a reaction to the severe cough she had at the time. Shortly after that my son was hospitalized for dehydration due to a prolonged fever. My husband stayed well but was exhausted taking care of the rest of the family. Within a few short months, misfortune seemed to be the only overshadowing presence in our home.

In the end, all of this loss was recoverable—I revived after months of physical therapy, my children got well, my husband got his wife and life back—but at the time, I had no indication that life would ever return to normal. For all I knew, I would be in bed the rest of my life. In fact, even after the physical pain subsided, the sense of loss (not only of what we had been through, but also our coming to terms with the possibility that it might never end) propelled me into depression. My body had recovered, but my soul still felt the loss. Even recoverable loss takes something away; it leaves you changed, less protected. It was nearly a year before life returned to a familiar routine.

Fred called immediately ("I received your letter and was distressed and just wanted to call you right away," said the message on my answering machine) and continued to call and write to me through this difficult time. "*I'm so proud of you,*" one of his letters said. "*The ordeal had to have been one of the toughest times of your life. (Just remembering it can bring tears.)*"

"When your heart can cry another's sadness . . ."

"*You were so helpful to the many who have been or are going through painful trials.*"

". . . then your heart is full of love."

"*I hope that the summer is a healing time for all of you. . . . Again, my thanks for remembering.*"

The summer was a healing time for us, but like most loss, it forced me to take a hard look at my life. In the end I wondered if my illness wasn't brought on by neglecting the first of Fred's spiritual toast sticks: taking time, slowing down, and incorporating silence into my life. I've often joked that the only thing that causes me to slow down is hitting a brick wall. I had been working full time from home since my children were born and was also trying to be a full-time mom. Colleagues would say I had the best of both worlds, but I also had the workload of both worlds. There was also a move and a transition to a new parish. My illness froze everything into a snapshot. I felt trapped, like Joseph in the cistern, dropped into an empty hole by his own brothers.

I thought a lot about Joseph as I began to recover and could think clearly for the first time in months. And upon revisiting his story—especially his plight in the cistern—I noticed something of God's goodness in it that I hadn't seen before. Cisterns are made to hold water, but there was no water in it at the time. Had there been, Joseph could have drowned. Instead he stayed relatively safe inside the cistern until his brothers inadvertently moved him toward his destiny in Egypt. Reflecting on my own cistern experience, I realized that God's intention was not to drown me, not to overwhelm me with illness, but only to hold me still for a while.

LOVE: STRONGER THAN ANYTHING

Fred knew how vulnerable people could be during loss. He sent me the Fra Giovanni quote to urge me to look for God's intent behind the struggle, because he knew that not everyone sees the "angel's hand" in loss. I think that's why he saw offering comfort as such an important way to carry out, practically, his love for his neighbor—because one of his "neighbors," a close friend who had struggled with emotional problems, wasn't able to see the angel's hand, couldn't understand that the cistern was only temporary.

"I wish he had been able to mourn whatever resentments he felt in this life," he said of his friend, "and eventually been able to recognize the great value he had for those who knew and loved him."

But his friend wasn't able to. One day while taping an episode of the *Neighborhood*, Fred received a call from the friend's wife. They hadn't seen each other for two years. Fred was told about his friend's nervous breakdown and subsequent hospitalization. He was eventually sent home with his medication, which he took all at once. After another stay in the hospital, he was sent home—inexplicably—with more pills. This time he rode his bike into the woods. His body was found three days later. "You know, Fred," his friend's wife had said, "he could never imagine that he was so much more than he thought he was."

Just a few months after his friend's death—and just before Easter—Fred received a package from his friend's wife. Carefully wrapped in tissue paper was a handcrafted wooden cross the friend had made. Upon it lay Jesus, whose face showed some of the abandonment Fred's friend may have felt while he made it. Jesus is able to relate human suffering to the Godhead, Fred had told me in one of our phone conversations during this time, because He Himself had endured it.

Fred treasured the gift even as he mourned the loss of his friend: "All I could think of as I looked at that gift was God, the source of all forgiveness and love, rising from the tomb waiting for all of us to recognize that love is stronger than anything, stronger even than death."

Even death, the greatest of the irreversible losses.

CHAPTER 9

HEADING TOWARD HEAVEN

Frankly, I think that after we die, we have this wide
understanding of what's real. And we'll probably say,
"Ah, so that's what it was all about."

FRED ROGERS

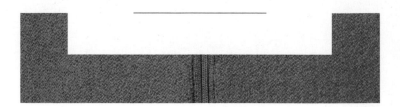

Ten years ago my father sent me a print of a Danny Hahlbohm painting for Christmas. The painting was titled "Reunion," but my dad liked to call it, "I'm Coming Home, Jesus." In the painting, Jesus is welcoming a man into heaven. With eyes closed, He enshrouds the man in a warm embrace. A dove hovers above the two, and two large hands rise out of the clouds they stand on, protectively cupping their embrace; the Father, the Son, and the Holy Spirit all rejoicing in the homecoming.

I was very moved by Dad's gift, which doesn't quite explain why it spent most of the next ten years in a box in the attic. It's not that I didn't like the painting; it's just that I didn't like to think about the day when my father would be the man in the picture. I didn't like to think about heaven, because to do so meant first having to think about death.

I pulled the print out of a box in the attic six months ago; I had to dig to find it among the mismatched curtains, discarded knickknacks, and framed photos I had no place to hang. My dad had just been diagnosed with lung cancer, and now I didn't have a choice but to confront his "coming home." I felt twice orphaned at the thought of losing Fred, in many ways my spiritual father, and then my dad, my earthly father, so close together. "If you react like this to Mister Rogers' death," Dad once chided me on the phone, "how will you react when I die?" Only too soon, I would find out.

WHAT IS ESSENTIAL

Fred kept a reminder of heaven too, but he didn't hide it in a box in the attic. Instead it held a prominent place in his office at the WQED building in Pittsburgh. The reminder was one of his favorite sayings, a framed copy of a quote from Antoine de Saint-Exupéry's *The Little Prince*, in its original French. It read: "*L'essentiel est invisible pour les yeux.*" What is essential is invisible to the eye.

While Fred spent most of his life quoting those words and imprinting them into his own life (they found their way into speeches, letters, and even his songs for the Neighborhood, one of which asks, "What do you think is important, really? What is essential for you and your neighbor?"), I think he knew that their full realization would only be possible in one place, that final trolley stop.

Fred was once asked whether he thought the Neighborhood was a metaphor for heaven. He answered that it was not his intention to make the Neighborhood a utopia, a "Pollyannish state." His television neighbors and the residents of the Neighborhood of Make-Believe dealt with real issues like death and divorce and real feelings like anger and fear. That's not how he pictured heaven: "When

I think about heaven," he said, "it is a state in which we are so greatly loved that there is no fear and doubt and disillusionment and anxiety. It is where people really do look at you with those eyes of Jesus."[1] Eyes that see what is wonderful about our neighbor. Eyes that can *see* the invisible, the essential in one another.

While the Neighborhood wasn't a metaphor for heaven, a few of the program episodes did have an otherworldly feel to them. In one series of shows, a star visitor, a puppet creature from the night sky, lands in the Neighborhood of Make-Believe, but he speaks a language of "me's" and "thee's" that neither the puppets nor the grownups are able to understand. What they are able to sense is that, as time passes, the star visitor begins to feel very sad about something. Finally, Daniel Striped Tiger, Fred Rogers' sensitive alter ego, is able to translate the strange tongue into a reason for the star visitor's sadness: he is enjoying his sojourn in the Neighborhood of Make-Believe but knows he will have to go back to his star when the night is over.

Daniel tells him that while he can't be in two places at once, he can think of his friends above when he is in the Neighborhood, and when he goes back home, he can think of his friends on earth below. When the program transitions back to Mister Rogers, he says that the biggest surprise for him was that Daniel was able to understand the star visitor. He was able to do so, Mister Rogers concludes, because "he was listening with his heart."

Again the influence of Saint-Exupéry's classic fable is

evident. Just like the Little Prince, the star visitor has fallen out of the heavens, an "alien" in a strange land. In Saint-Exupéry's tale, the Little Prince travels from planet to planet, observing adults doing "serious" (and usually futile) grown-up things. Then he lands on earth, where he happens upon a pilot whose plane has been downed in the middle of the Sahara Desert. He tells the pilot of his previous adventures, including meeting a lonely little fox with a bit of advice: "Here is my secret," the fox tells the Little Prince, offering his words as a gift. "It's quite simple: It is only with the heart that one can see rightly; what is essential is invisible to the eye."[2] And Daniel Striped Tiger uncovers that secret when he is able to translate the essential in his own star visitor by "listening with his heart."

CHILDREN'S SPECIAL CONNECTION TO GOD

The fact that Fred Rogers used this quote from *The Little Prince* as his personal mantra is not surprising to me. If I am convinced of anything, it is that there was a Little Prince in Mister Rogers. They both embodied the innocence and wonder and ingenuousness of childhood, and they both shared similar missions. Mister Rogers came for a time to rouse what was dormant in us "serious" adults, teaching us to appreciate life's mysteries through the eyes of a child, because he never lost the ability to look through those eyes. His ministry wasn't solely to children; of course, children needed encouragement to continue in what was already natural to them, but it was their parents who needed to see anew.

Fred once told me a story that I know he liked to repeat often. "I heard this true story of this child, a little four-year-old boy whose mother and dad had just brought home a baby sister," he said. "Sound familiar to you?" Then he laughed. I had almost the identical scenario at home when Fred and I first met. "He pleaded with his mother and dad to have some private time with this baby; in fact, insisted. Well, the mother and dad were concerned; they thought maybe he was planning to hurt that baby. Finally he won. And he walked into the baby's room, and the mother and dad thought, 'We will just stay at the door to be sure that the baby is safe.' The little boy simply walked up to the crib, looked at the baby, and said, 'Tell me what it was like, I'm beginning to forget.' Out of the mouths of babes, you know. So heaven doesn't have any boundaries."

Fred's story is an echo of William Wordsworth's sober observation in his "Intimations of Immortality from Recollections of Early Childhood":

> *Heaven lies about us in our infancy!*
> *Shades of the prison-house begin to close*
> *Upon the growing boy.*

Fred was trying to preserve that special connection that children have with God, their absolute trust and acceptance, and at the same time, he was trying to loose their parents from the prison-house. For Fred, the prison-house included the "stuff" that we collect to fill up our lives, things like new cars and new houses that have left us empty as we've grown and matured into "adults" just like the ones the Little Prince met along the way.

After his encounter with the stranded pilot, the Little Prince, like Daniel's star visitor, must return home. ("It'll look as if I'm dead," he tells the pilot, "and that won't be true."[3]) At Fred's memorial service, his friend Saleem Ghubril, executive director of the Pittsburgh Project, told a story about one evening when students from the faith-based outreach program were to perform. The children knew that Mister Rogers was supposed to attend. So as not to draw attention away from the children, Fred and Joanne sneaked in through a side entrance. After the program began, one of the children, unable to contain the excitement of the moment, peered out into the dark audience and shouted, "Where you at, Mister Rogers? Where you at?" After finishing the story, Saleem said, "Today, I have absolutely no question as to Mister Rogers' whereabouts."

And neither should we; Mister Rogers is home.

OUR IDEA OF HEAVEN

Once our idea of heaven meant
all the dead relatives waiting
on the kept lawn of the many mansions
as if, suddenly sinless, they had nothing to do.

Deborah Digges, in her poem "Custody"

Until recently, I never thought much about whether those who go on to heaven still have a connection with those of us left behind. Of course I know that all believers will one day be reunited in heaven, but it's never been a part of my theology to think that people in heaven somehow help those of us here on earth like some newly commissioned guardian angels, or at the very least, inspire us in our daily lives. But maybe that's because until recently, I didn't have a reason to hope for a connection.

I think Fred felt that loved ones in heaven *do* help those they left behind. He once told me, "I think of my mother and my dad, and they're both in heaven and have been for a long time, and I know that they still love me and they help me. I have friends who are in heaven, and I know that they inspire me to do all kinds of things in this life."

His friend Henri Nouwen would agree. In *Finding My Way Home*, Henri wrote, "After a very short visit to earth the time comes for each of us to pass from this world to the next . . . and we leave the world for full communion with God. It is possible for us, like Jesus, to send our spirit of love to our friends when we leave them. . . . It is our greatest gift for those we love."[4]

Perhaps the toast sticks for the hands, the practical out-working of our love for our neighbor, continue beyond this world. Maybe our idea of heaven, of those "waiting on the kept lawn of the many mansions as if, suddenly sinless, they had nothing to do," as Deborah Digges writes, is wrong. And maybe there is something recoverable in death after all; it may not be the greatest of the irreversible losses. Death may feel like an amputation at the time of the loss, but if the connection is still vibrant, perhaps those aren't phantom pains haunting us but the spirit of love.

Fred once told writer Tom Junod, who after writing an article on Fred for *Esquire* magazine became a close friend, "The connections we make in the course of a life, maybe that's what heaven is, Tom. We make so many connections here on earth."[5]

And in the literal heaven, those connections continue. At Fred's memorial service, we all stood and sang the first verse of his favorite hymn, William Walsham How's "For All the Saints":

For all the saints who from their labors rest,
Who Thee by faith before the world confessed,
Thy name, O Jesus, be forever blest.
Alleluia! Alleluia!

And then the fourth verse:

> *Oh, blest communion, fellowship divine,*
> *We feebly struggle, they in glory shine;*
> *Yet all are one within your great design.*
> *Alleluia! Alleluia!*

Yet all are one; that's our hope.

TOAST STICKS FOR THE HEART, EYES, AND HANDS

Fred once said that he loved being part of humanity, but he had lots of thoughts about what it would be like when he was gone. When I asked him what he meant, he said, "I think about what the next chapter will be like. Because [our time on earth] is such a little part of all of life. It's a wonderful part, it's a sad part, it's a joyous part, but it's just one part."

And that one part can make an enormous difference in the lives of others, especially when we commit to a life of spiritual wholeness that's represented by looking inward with our hearts (inner disciplines affect how we see others); looking outward with our eyes (how we see others affects how we treat others); and finally, by using what we've learned practically, with our hands.

ONE FINAL BROADCAST

Sometimes when people speak, the impact of their words is so strong and goes so deep that they seem to have a quality of eternity about them.

Thomas Moore, *The Soul's Religion*

The very last time I saw Fred in person, I asked him a question for no apparent reason, except perhaps out of idle curiosity. It didn't fit in with the rest of the interview or even the context of what we were talking about at the moment. In fact, I didn't even remember asking it until I looked back at the interview tape years later. Hearing his answer again, after his death, I found that his words had a "quality of eternity" about them, as if they were spoken from eternity and not from the conversation we happened to be having that day.

"If you had *one final broadcast*," I asked, "*one final opportunity* to address your television neighbors, and you could tell them the single most important lesson of your life, what would you say?"

He paused a moment and then said, ever so slowly:

Well, I would want [those] who were listening somehow to know that they had unique value, that there isn't anybody in the whole world exactly like them and that there never has been and there never will be.

And that they are loved by the Person who created them, in a unique way.

If they could know that and really know it and have that behind their eyes, they could look with those eyes on their neighbor and realize, "My neighbor has unique value too; there's never been anybody in the whole world like my neighbor, and there never will be." If they could value that person—if they could love that person—in ways that we know that the Eternal loves us, then I would be very grateful.

And I think that from where he sits in his new neighborhood, Mister Rogers is just that, eternally grateful.

EPILOGUE

But an inheritance is nothing we ask for or earn or deserve.
It is something we are given by the testator, and we can
either accept or betray the responsibility.

Madeleine L'Engle, *The Irrational Season*

I've had this quote by Madeleine L'Engle taped to my computer monitor since I began writing this book. There were others, too, to encourage me along the way. One was an excerpt from one of Fred's letters, which I photocopied so that it would be in his own hand: "*All that matters is your motives,*" it read in his precise, upright lettering. "*God will lead the way. You know that.*"

Another was a Scripture verse one of my college students sent me as an encouragement. I even taped up my own words from an article I had once written on Tolkien's *The Hobbit*: "Adventure can be scary and unpredictable, but the more you continue in it, the more you lose that sense of fear and doubt (and the less you care about being late for dinner). You begin to gather up your internal resources with confidence." But it was the Madeleine L'Engle quote that I looked to most often, because it described the main work of writing this book: accepting the responsibility to share a legacy.

At the time the idea for this book was being conceived, I ran across a Greek word that became especially significant to me in this regard. I have always liked to know the etymology of words, what languages they came from and any stories associated with their origin (another of the natural instincts I share with Fred to dig below the surface of things). The word I unearthed was *trust*, but the Greek language translates it as "deposit." In fact, what prompted my interest in the word was the apostle Paul's admonition to Timothy to "guard what has been entrusted to your care" (1 Timothy 6:20). What was entrusted to Timothy's care was the Christian faith, and the word used to describe that entrusting was *deposit*.

The word *deposit* is very similar to the concept of inheritance or legacy. After poring over some of my husband's theological books, I found the following description: "The word is *paratheke*, which means *a deposit committed to someone's trust*. A man might deposit something with a friend to be kept for his children or his loved ones; he might deposit his valuables in a temple for safekeeping, for the temples were the banks of the ancient world. In each case the thing deposited was a *paratheke*. In the ancient world there was no more sacred duty than the safeguarding of such a deposit and the returning of it when in due time it was claimed."[1]

Digging deeper, I found that the biblical concept of deposit was also examined by fifth-century monk Vincent of Lerins, in a most lyrical way:

> What is meant by deposit? that is, that which is committed to thee, not that which is invented of thee; that which thou hast received, not that which thou hast devised . . . a thing brought to thee, not brought forth of thee; wherein thou must not be an author, but a keeper. . . . that which is committed to thee, let that remain with thee, and that deliver. Thou hast received gold, render then gold.[2]

My sincerest hope is that I have taken what has been entrusted to me and rendered it back just as I received it, as gold.

NOTES

Introduction:
The Real Mister Rogers

1. Nor have I ever heard the first President George Bush say, "It wouldn't be prudent at this juncture," but that didn't stop Dana Carvey from immortalizing him that way. Interestingly enough, Dana Carvey came up with his George Bush impersonation by combining two of his other characters: John Wayne—and Mister Rogers.

2. The network mercifully sent me as the interviewer in part because it was my idea, I had already watched the show daily with my son for an entire year, and I had worked on securing the interview. The only other interview of this kind I conducted during my eight years in television there was another interview with Fred Rogers.

3. Rev. Gordon McClellan, "Interview: Fred Rogers," *Christian Networks Journal*, June 2001.

4. Reporter Bob Faw, *NBC Nightly News*, February 27, 2003.

5. Don Feder, "It's a Psychobabble Day in the Neighborhood," *Virginian-Pilot and Ledger-Star*, October 17, 1994.

6. James Kaplan, "The Good Neighbor," *TV Guide*, October 26–November 1, 1996.

7. Jessica Reaves, "I Was Mister Rogers' Neighbor," *Time* Online Edition, February 27, 2003, http://www.time.com/time/sampler/article/0,8599,88632,00.html.

8. Dietrich Bonhoeffer, *Letters and Papers From Prison* (Riverside, NJ: Simon & Schuster, 1997), 347.

9. Ironically, a year after the book's publication, its author, a pilot like the narrator of his classic fable, embarked on a World War II spy mission for the Allies and disappeared somewhere over the Mediterranean. He was never seen again. While I was writing this chapter, a report was issued stating that, after sixty years of searching, Saint-Exupéry's plane was finally found and identified.

10. Antoine de Saint-Exupéry, *The Little Prince* (San Diego: Harcourt, 1943), 78.

11. Ibid., 77.

Chapter 1.
The Importance of Taking Time,
The Importance of Silence

1. Jeanne Marie Laskas, "The Good Life—and Works—of Mister Rogers," *Life*, November 1992.

2. A year after Fred Rogers' death, the Pittsburgh Symphony Orchestra performed a tribute titled "The Music of Fred Rogers." The event, which I attended with my husband and children, beautifully illustrated two of Fred's most important themes by utilizing this song. One of the performers pretends to be frustrated with another performer who likes to "take his time." She belts out, "What Do You Do (with the Mad That You Feel)?" while he counters with, "I Like to Take My Time." Fred would have been pleased that the program was able to integrate his message to share feelings with his equally important emphasis on "taking your time."

3. Fred appeared on *The Tonight Show* three times, with Johnny Carson as host (September 4, 1980), Joan Rivers as host (April 29, 1986), and Jay Leno as host (January 16, 1989). *The Tonight Show* highlight comes from Peter David, "Do You Feel Bad? That's Okay." Peter David's other memory of Mister Rogers came about when he wrote an op-ed piece for the

New York Times about the time he couldn't get a Cabbage Patch doll for his then–six-year-old daughter. He mentioned Mister Rogers in the piece, and shortly after it was published a package arrived from Mister Rogers' office, addressed to his daughter, with a signed photo and a Mister Rogers' T-shirt.

4. L. K. Friedrich and A. H. Stein, "Aggressive and Prosocial Television Programs and the Natural Behavior of Preschool Children," *Monographs of the Society for the Research in Child Development* 38, no. 4 (1973).

5. Tom Peters and Robert Waterman, *In Search of Excellence: Lessons from America's Best-Run Companies* (New York: Harper & Row, 1982).

6. C. S. Lewis, *The Screwtape Letters* (Uhrichsville, OH: Barbour & Company, 1985), 90.

7. Ibid., 20.

8. Fred Rogers, in an interview with Rev. Gordon McClellan, *Christian Networks Journal*, June 2001.

9. Fred Rogers, "In the Journey, We Need Friends," in Christopher de Vinck, *Nouwen Then* (Grand Rapids, MI: Zondervan, 1999), 77.

10. Ibid., 78.

Chapter 2.
A Presence Transformed by Prayer

1. Friedrich Nietzsche wrote in *Thus Spake Zarathustra* (1891), "It is however a shame to pray! Not for all, but for thee, and me, and whoever hath his conscience in his head."

2. Professional wrestler turned governor Jesse Ventura told *Playboy* magazine in its November 1999, issue: "Organized religion is a sham and a crutch for weak-minded people who need strength in numbers."

3. Alexander Pope, "An Essay on Man: Epistle II," lines 277–79.

Chapter 3.
The Wondrous Work of the Holy Spirit

1. Cathy Larson Sky, "Love Letter to My Neighbor," *(Chapel Hill, NC) News and Observer*, November 18, 2003.

Chapter 4.
The Best Gift: Your Honest Self

1. Jeanne Marie Laskas, "The Good Life—and Works— of Mister Rogers," *Life*, November 1992.

2. Macker's Web blog, "To Live on His Block," February 27, 2003, Fourth Age Communications.

3. Jump the Shark, *Mister Rogers' Neighborhood*, http://jumptheshark.com.

4. Ibid.

5. Madeleine L'Engle, *The Irrational Season* (New York: Seabury Press, 1977), 76.

6. Interview by Nöel Tolentino, Bunnyhop e-zine, http://www2.norwich.edu/pferreir/Rogers%20Intervi ew.doc.

7. C. S. Lewis, *The Screwtape Letters* (Uhrichsville, OH: Barbour & Company, 1985), 54.

8. Ibid.

Chapter 5.
Who Is My Neighbor?

1. *The Holy Rule of St. Benedict*, 1949 edition, trans. Rev. Boniface Verheyen, OSB.

2. Frederick Buechner, *Listening to Your Life* (San Francisco: HarperSanFrancisco, 1992), x.

3. Madeleine L'Engle, *A Wind in the Door* (New York: Farrar Straus & Giroux, 1973), 97.

4. Ibid., 99.

5. Ibid., 98.

6. Ibid., 99.

Chapter 6.
The Power of Forgiveness

1. Joseph Cardinal Bernardin, *The Gift of Peace: Personal Reflections* (Chicago: Loyola Press, 1997), 82–83.

2. Ibid., 65.

3. Ibid., 49.

Chapter 8.
Difficult Times

1. Douglas Anderson, "Mister Rogers' Neighborhood Watch," http://www.geocities.com/SunsetStrip/Alley/-7028/mrnw.htm. Italics added.

Chapter 9.
Heading Toward Heaven

1. Fred Rogers, quoted in Wendy Murray Zoba, "Won't You Be My Neighbor?" *Christianity Today*, March 2000.

2. Antoine de Saint-Exupéry, *The Little Prince* (San Diego: Harcourt, 1943), 63.

3. Ibid., 78.

4. Henri Nouwen, *Finding My Way Home* (New York: The Crossroad Publishing Company, 2001), 138-139.

5. Tom Junod, "Can You Say . . . Hero?" *Esquire*, November 1998.

Epilogue

1. William Barclay, *The Letters to Timothy, Titus, and Philemon* (Philadelphia: Westminster Press, 1975), 151.
2. John Henry Newman, *Historical Sketches*, Volume 1 (London: Logmans, Green, and Co., 1908), 388.